FIND A FORTUNE

CD
DB
DO
EG

12

FIND A FORTUNE

How to Buy, Sell and Make Money on eBay and at Boot Sales

LORNE SPICER

ORION

A CIP catalogue record for this book is available
from the British Library.

ISBN: 0 75286 958 2

Printed in Great Britain by
Clays Ltd, St Ives plc

The publisher and author also wish to thank the following for
permission to reproduce images: Abbey Antiques, Henry Aldridge Auctioneers,
The House of Portia, Vectis Auctions and Watch This Space UK Limited.

Every effort has been made to fulfil requirements with regard to
reproducing copyright material. The author and publisher will be glad to
rectify any omissions at the earliest opportunity.

www.orionbooks.co.uk

CONTENTS

ACKNOWLEDGEMENTS

Thanks must go to:

The 1987 hurricane, without which Peter and Eileen Stevenson would never have seen their nursery business destroyed and had the brilliant idea of replacing it with a boot sale.

Standard Chartered Bank for providing my husband with so much overtime that every Sunday I was free to trail around Essex gathering car booty.

Mr H and Mr O for the endless fun, quips and stories that brightened up every boot sale we filmed at.

Tracy for filling in the gaps in my life, for organising my life and for her endless enthusiasm.

Ally Sharman, Ally's mum, Dom and Jay for having faith in the fact that boot sales are brilliant viewing.

Leopard Films – James, Bernard and all the directors, crew and production staff – and of course Mr Mark Franks who has elevated my status from Queen of Collectables to Lady Lorne.

Orion – Ian, Laura and Luigi for 'getting it' and making this book a reality.

Nicola and NCI for putting up with my endless stream of 'suggestions' and acting on them.

Mum, Dad and Chard for never quite converting to car boots but supporting everything, always 100%.

Martin – the love of my life – and car boot convert for all his boot sale bargains and Essex boy philosophy on life.

Everyone, everywhere who knows the sound of the 5 a.m. boot sale alarm and to the next generation of boot sale babies, especially the best boy in the whole wide world:

Little Man Dan
'Does your mummy work at boot sales too...?'

INTRODUCTION

I'm writing this book surrounded by car booty, specialist collectors' guides, empty packing boxes, bags of polystyrene chips and bubble wrap – and this is just my spare room. If I included the items in the loft, which I can't actually get into now, the garage, which obviously has no room for my car, and the two lock-ups that are costing me £60 a month then I would probably be able to spend the next ten years listing items on eBay!

And all this started seventeen years ago when I passed a field in Basildon, Essex, where hundreds of people were standing in the freezing cold with tables full of stuff and hundreds more were walking up and down carrying bags of shopping! Out of curiosity I stopped and joined the throngs of people and some five hours later returned home amazed at the amount of stuff I had bought for next to nothing. Now hooked on the early starts, freezing cold and bland black coffee, the trip became a weekly source of pleasure until, by 1992, it was inevitable that I had to clear out and sell some stuff myself as we were about to move home. After one morning I was £286 richer and couldn't believe my luck.

What really started as a private club for those who dared venture out and trawl a lot of rubbish in search of that one item that just might be the bargain of a lifetime, has developed into an enormous business. Certainly boot sales in my neck of the woods boomed during the 1990s recession, which saw many people in Essex facing the repossession of their homes and bankruptcies at an all-time high. Given that most self-employed workers found they were not eligible for state benefits, and with building work and many other types of jobs drying up, selling possessions at boot sales became, for many people in the county, the only way to make ends meet or to get any form of income. Many of these people never actually returned to traditional work, opting instead for the independence of life as a trader, while others simply opt in during the summer months when the weather is good or during the school holidays when it's time to clear the kids' old toys and clothes before another school year sets in.

For me, the thrill of the boot sale never, ever recedes. I've filmed at more than 300 boot sales from Clitheroe in Lancashire to Penrith in Cumbria, to Ford near Arundel in West Sussex, to Bristol, Colchester, Kent, West Wycombe, and back to Stevenson's Farm in Essex. It doesn't matter how many times you visit the same boot sale it will always be different – a different atmosphere, different buyers and different items. Where one week I can come home laden with toys or books, at the same venue the next week it could be designer clothes and a

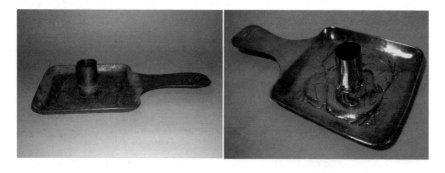

This Arts and Crafts Newlyn School candlestick cost 50p at a boot sale and, after being cleaned, sold for £170 on eBay.

pub bar stool shaped like a pint of Guinness! And there's still plenty to be found – last year, we bought an old candlestick which looked like nothing special but, in fact, was made by the Newlyn School – the renowned Arts and Crafts era metalware producers. It cost just 50p at the boot sale, and then was resold on eBay where it made £170. Not a fortune, but certainly a healthy return. Most people know that they are unlikely to find a priceless Ming vase at a boot sale, but there is a good chance that they could find an old candlestick for 50p that makes £170. If I can do it – anyone can!

The good news for me is that I am not alone. There's hardly any concrete research on just how popular boot sales are or just what sort of economy exists as a result of these events. Mintel undertook a survey in 1996 and discovered that around 15% of people go to a boot sale at least once a month, generating £673m worth of sales – and that was nine years ago. The same report forecast sales of £794m by the year 2000, but in truth the figure is likely to be well in excess of £1bn a year today. Mintel added that it had calculated some 15,000 car boot sales took place across the country every week, attracting 250,000 sellers and 2.5 million visitors and buyers. Since this time, boot sales have grown and grown and seem to be taking over just about every vacant field that adjoins a major road in the summer months. Given that Mintel has not conducted any update since this first survey, any estimates of just what the boot-sale business involves now can be only guesswork.

My own view is that in this time boot sales have grown between five and tenfold. When I wrote the proposal for the *Boot Sale Challenge* programme, it was based purely on my own experiences and commissioned by London Weekend Television as a small fill-in regional programme for the Sunday

evening 6 p.m. slot. No one could have foreseen the cult viewing that followed or the endless re-commissions which resulted
in some 150 programmes being made and broadcast from London to Australia, Tenerife and France! Since then, there have
been all sorts of programmes made which are variations on the
Boot Sale Challenge theme including my own *Car Booty* programme for BBC1, which staggered many at the Beeb with a
huge audience share. More than 2 million people tune in every
day, making it the most watched programme across the five
channels in its timeslot.

Of course, television programmes on collecting, antiques,
auctions and boot sales help generate interest and reflect the
real lives of the people enjoying this potentially profitable
hobby, but I firmly believe that what makes boot sales such a
must is the instinctive gene in all of us to find a bargain – something that we buy and then discover is worth a fortune! The
great thing with boot sales, of course, is that most people who
go to them have had good buys: items that they have bought
after searching for such an example for years or a bargain buy
that they have sold on at a profit. Some have had incredible
buys, and it is these that further fuel the interest and the drive to
traipse out to yet another boot sale on yet another dark, damp
Sunday morning just in case there's a fortune out there to be
found.

What has changed so dramatically since boot sales began is
the access to potential buyers who will pay £170 for a candlestick – and that has come through www.ebay.com. The website
is now regularly hitting the headlines for its weird and wacky
sales – from Tesco carrier bags making nearly £5 to bottled
water from the Princess Diana Memorial Fountain selling for
£248 and pieces of toast reportedly bearing the image of the

Virgin Mary realising nearly £300. For the rest of us, here is an instant worldwide market through which to sell all those boot sale buys and there's no doubt a lot of people are making a lot of money from spotting niches in the market where they can buy items cheaply at boot sales and sell them on eBay for a profit; after all, 15 million bids are placed worldwide on eBay each day and eBay users account for a third of all British Internet traffic.

Don't just take my word for it – Richard Franklin, boot sale organiser, who runs four car boot sale sites and the car-booters' bible, *The Car Boot Calendar*, explains:

The heyday of boot sales was the early to mid-nineties but luckily no one seems to have noticed. As the real, collectable bargains have become scarcer and scarcer I expected the dealers to evaporate but on the whole they are still there, still hoping to pick up some decent pieces for pennies even though almost every week they moan that they can't find anything! As long as High Street consumerism remains rampant car boot sales will flourish. People's houses are simply not big enough to store everything they buy and for most people they are a pleasurable day out and a way to get rid of clutter. eBay has been a huge boost to car boot sales, inspiring a whole new generation of people to try their hand at buying and selling and, for the buying, car boot sales have to be the first port of call.

And it's not just eBay that is booming. There are all the ancillary services building businesses off the back of eBay. From storage companies offering to store unwanted items for a small rental fee, to Royal Mail which estimates it will have delivered

55 million items ordered online in 2004 compared with 40 million in 2003 and 20 million in 2002. As Gary Waring, who runs Abbey Antiques and now has a £1.5m turnover thanks to eBay, explains, 'eBay has opened up a whole host of business potentials with people making livings out of selling ancillary items such as bubble wrap and packing.'

Think of the American Gold Rush in the 1800s where thousands sought their fortune from the hills and valleys digging for gold nuggets and the number who succeeded probably compares to the amount of lottery winners worldwide. However, the people who really made the money were the ones who built up businesses supporting the treasure seekers: the ironmongers, the brothel owners, the spade and axe makers and a certain Levi Strauss – an immigrant who arrived in the US and founded his company in 1873 supplying his denim to others on the Gold Rush trail. A pair of Levi jeans made £17,000 on eBay. They were found in a pile of mud four years ago in an old silver-mining town in Nevada and are thought to date from around 1880. Considered to be in fair condition despite having some holes, several rips and being very faded, they are thought to be the oldest pair of jeans in the world, hence the price realised. But even the price paid for these jeans pales in comparison to the money made by the Levi Strauss company itself over the years. Who is best off? The Gold Rusher who never made a mint, the person who discovered the oldest pair of Levi jeans and sold them, or the man who spotted a gap in the market and founded a company on the back of the Gold Rush and never had to lift a shovel again!

This book is your guide to the twenty-first-century Gold Rush. Using the advice and tips of hundreds of eBayers, car-booters and my own experience, this guide will ensure that you can turn your life around either by becoming the best bargain hunter and profit turner on the Internet, or by spotting a new niche market that just could see you building an international business of eBay proportions! Whatever you do – enjoy it! And remember there's always a boot sale bargain out there!

CHAPTER ONE

CASHING IN YOUR CLUTTER

Personally, I have no idea why I suddenly spot something on an antiques stand, a boot sale stall or a skip and find myself driven by the need to acquire it. Actually, that's not quite true – in the case of items in skips it's very often because I just can't bear to see something being discarded, chucked and destined for a landfill site that could so easily be used either for its original purpose or, with a bit of TLC, turned into something else just as useful. Yet, this does not explain the need to part with hard-earned cash for something that I don't need, already have, or simply find cute, interesting, wacky or curious.

In December 1998 Bonhams (formerly Phillips) the auction house managed £20,000, double the estimate, for a rare English Delft cup bought at a boot sale in 1996 for just £3.

I have worked with many cameramen and sound guys who, despite my best efforts to convert them to collecting and appreciating the craftsmanship that is often found in older items, simply look blank. However, several boot sales later and the same cameramen can often be found with sets of golf clubs in the boot of his car or old cameras piling up in the footwell. Now, it might be a case of 'if you can't beat them join them', but I actually believe it's simply a matter of finding which button to press that makes individuals suddenly switch on to the excitement of a bargain find or an object of interest, or *vertu* to use the auction-house term. Of course, a lot of people will tell you that they don't collect as such, but believe me, one example of an item is fine, two is arguably a pair but thereafter and it's a collection.

In 2001 Sotheby's in Billingshurst, Sussex, sold an oil painting found rolled up in a garage which made £55,200. The painting, by an important Victorian landscape painter, Sidney Richard Percy, was discovered by the vendor when he moved into his new home, tucked away at the back of the garage and it nearly ended up on the bonfire before being identified by a Sotheby's expert.

So, whatever psychology is at work, there are two main forces driving our nation's hoarding – the first is simple accumulation, either through the nesting instinct or to establish status, something we see all the time within the car market, of course. Second, there's the bargain gene – the idea of getting something for a lot less than it should be bought for, or purchasing an item that simply through age has more panache, craftsmanship, quality and class than its modern equivalent.

Christie's in 1999 managed £58,748 for a collection of seven posters by Alphonse Mucha discovered rolled up in a coach house in the south of England.

Collecting has often been a symbol of wealth. The grand tours of the eighteenth century involved young men touring the world, and Europe in particular, and bringing back all sorts of souvenirs ranging from Roman statues to Egyptian mummies and lion skins – all were trophies that indicated not only a gentleman's wealth but also his standing, influence and knowledge. My grandparents were nowhere near this category and thought they'd made it because they were able to support their families, bring them up and pay for their own funerals. Then there's my parents' generation, who struggled to save a deposit for a house, shunned credit and finance and can't quite believe their luck that their properties are worth such considerable sums today. They are the first of the working-class families to actually have had the money and education to appreciate antiques, design and 'nice things'. Many have been in a position in later life to indulge their childhood fantasies and buy Hornby railways, Steiff bears and porcelain dolls, and tin toys of the quality they remember seeing in toy shops and department stores but would rarely have been able to receive as a present. Now all this is understandable, excusable and relatively logical, so where does collecting get out of hand and clutter take on a whole new form of its own that suddenly starts controlling people and their lives?

In 2001 Sotheby's in Sussex sold a Minton majolica punch bowl which had been used by the vendor, Elizabeth Wallace, for her dog Mandy's biscuits. It made £5,000.

Clutter is simply the dust that has gathered through our lives, experiences, jobs, homes and relationships that for some reason we are unable to wipe away. A collection has purpose, clutter simply overwhelms us and in some cases to such an extent that lives become totally inhibited, relationships shatter and our focus on everyday life distorts. So why not just make a decision to clear the decks of clutter, dump the lot and be done with it? Well, for many people clutter provides a security blanket of sorts, a cushion from having to deal with other issues. If I clear all the clutter, I might regret it or I will have to redecorate because I'll be able to see how outdated the decor has become. More importantly today is the worrying issue that dumping clutter might involve unsuspectingly abandoning a priceless piece that could have provided a real cash nest egg. In reality most of us know that the chances of finding that elusive object is about the same as winning the lottery – but hey, someone has to find it or win it! Would you throw £2, £20, £200 or even £2,000 down the drain? If someone handed you any of these sums with no strings attached, wouldn't it make your day? Well, that's exactly why most people are so paranoid about clearing out the clutter and that's why we are going to look at cashing in the clutter rather than clearing it.

Where to Start

Don't think of the task as clearing your clutter but as a job that will result in you counting your cash! Planning is the key. It's easy to start a clear-out and soon find that your entire home looks as if a bomb has hit it and you cannot see the wood for the trees. First things first:

🐷 Be realistic about just how much clutter you have and how long it might take to go through everything and get it sorted.

🐷 Work out the hours likely to be needed and decide how best to find time for the clear-out.

🐷 Consider taking the time off from work or setting aside an entire weekend to get the task completed.

🐷 Enlist the help of friends and family to aid with the hard graft – but organise them properly, giving each separate tasks so their time isn't wasted.

🐷 Consider disposing of the real rubbish in the most environmentally friendly way, i.e. glass to glass-recycling bins, clothes to charity shops, newspapers tied up and ready for collection.

🐷 Have a camera to hand to photograph items that you feel may need to be valued or simply those that you are disposing of but which have some sort of emotional meaning for you. It's also well worthwhile to take snaps of the rooms you are clearing before and after, so you have a record of what you have achieved and can keep yourself in check in future and make sure you never return to the clutter of your previous life.

🐷 Have a notebook or dictaphone handy so you can keep a running record of what items need to be valued, what is going to the charity shops, in the skip or to the boot sale.

🐷 Get some strong indelible marker pens so each box or bag packed can be easily identified. Avoid using any ink that could run if it gets wet, as you could arrive at a rainy boot sale and find that all your efforts to label everything properly have simply smudged in the rain.

Contact your local council to find out what advice they can offer on the disposal of certain items. Some councils will collect and dispose of old fridges and freezers for you; others have environmentally friendly recycling schemes for books and old newspapers and can give you details of collection or drop-off points. Bottle-bank schemes and in some cases plastic bottle and tin recycling bin bags can be provided, helping the local dustmen dispose of your rubbish in a more efficient manner.

Ask local charity shops what they are interested in taking and what they cannot accommodate before you start your clear-out, as this will save you a lot of bother later on. Many charity shops do have volunteers who will come and collect larger items from you, particularly furniture, providing it meets current fire and safety regulations. Others will ask for clothes to be presentable, wearable and preferably washed and ironed, while some have the facilities to wash and iron clothes in the charity shop's backroom. Either way, Help the Aged recently announced that it has to pay councils £300,000 a year to dispose of goods left by the public that are impossible to sell.

A lady bought a brooch from a charity shop in the north of England for 50p, which was later sold at Phillips in London for £13,225. The vendor, who remained anonymous, said, 'I have always loved scouring markets and second-hand shops, but this really was a huge unexpected bonus.'

One of my three lock-ups – time to rent another one!

Clearing a Room

Allocate one room or space in your home as the one that will be cleared completely. This is central HQ for the clear-out operation and only the items that are definitely going to be either kept or sold are to go in here.

Make sure there are areas within the room where only items for a boot sale, or potentially an auction specialist, or eBay listings are to be put.

If you already have an idea of any of these items' values or the price that you would want for them at a boot sale, consider pricing each item as you go along.

You'll run out of space more quickly than you think so try to have plenty of table or shelf space available in this room so that you can make use of the space by 'stacking' items rather than just having lots of stuff on the floor.

Don't cut corners – if something is worth selling it's worth taking the time to wrap it and pack it properly to avoid damage and/or disaster during the clear-out.

So have plenty of bubble wrap and boxes at hand – newspaper is fine but can rub off onto your hands and the items and it will never protect as well as bubble wrap, which can be purchased in large rolls from most storage companies or stationery specialists. Similarly, most local supermarkets simply dump their boxes into skips for recycling at the back of the store but if you ask, most will keep the larger, most sturdy boxes aside for you to collect.

Be realistic about the amount of stuff you have and consider hiring a skip to dispose of the real rubbish. True, this involves a cost, but then endless trips backwards and forwards to the dump will eat into your time and cost in terms of petrol too.

An original menu card celebrating the last trip of Scott of the Antarctic was discovered behind a painting recovered from an old skip and made £6,500 at Christie's in 1999.

Tackling the Clutter

Don't be daunted by the task and tempted to simply start moving boxes of clutter from one room to another because you'll never get anywhere. Ruthlessness is the key – you must remove any sentimentality or attachment from these items and view them much less as personal possessions and much more as hard cash that needs to be realised. So:

Do make sure that the items you are clearing are yours! If you have 'borrowed' something or are clearing a house following a death in the family these are testing times and it's important to check with everyone that they are happy for the items to be sold. There's nothing worse than clearing a house only to discover that certain members of the family have taken offence that Aunty Hilda's cracked teapot without a lid has been dumped when Little George would have loved to have had it as a memento.

Don't overlook anything at all, from the curtains to the chandelier, the light fittings to the fireplace – every nook and cranny should be checked and explored and by the end of the day all the cupboards should be bare because anything you want to keep will have been placed in the 'clear room' for safe-keeping and anything you want to sell will have been placed in the clear room ready for sale.

If you find yourself taking hours deciding whether to keep or sell something then you need to buck up! Allow yourself to keep just five items of 'clutter' from each room – this will soon focus the mind and make you concentrate on what you *really, really* want and before you know it you will realise that, in fact, most of this stuff has been bought with the justification that one day it would provide a nice little nest egg – and that's what you are now doing!

Don't let your personal taste dictate the potential saleability of an item – true, the 1970s flared orange trousers may not be something that you would consider wearing but if they have an Ozzie Clark label in they certainly have a value so they will need to be checked not chucked.

Don't be ridiculous about certain items – providing you have followed the guide so far, use an element of common sense so that if something is shattered into a thousand pieces, rusted beyond use, no longer any good for serving its original purpose or is simply rubbish – dump it.

Contact charity shops regarding items that you may not wish to sell personally at a boot sale or auction but feel others may have a use for. I will never sell my old shoes or any electrical equipment but many charity shops will take shoes and have qualified electrician volunteers who will rewire old electrical equipment properly so that it can be resold.

Oxfam in Reading took a pair of donated paintings which it had failed to sell at £25 in one of their shops to Dreweatt Neate and they realised £3,200 at the Reading auction house.

Check cases, boxes, pockets, tins, etc to make sure that they are empty and do not contain any hidden treasure before you sell them or that there are no personal contact details, receipts, etc if they are charity-shop bound.

In 2000 Spink auctioneers in London realised £40,250 for a £100 banknote dated 12 October 1790. The rarity of the note itself was overshadowed by the fact that the vendor had discovered it hidden in a secret compartment of a desk that he had bought six months earlier from an antiques shop for just £500.

Personal papers, bills, receipts and records all need to be kept for six years if you are self-employed but, for the rest of the population, can be destroyed. However, given the level of fraud around today it's sensible to dispose of these in a fitting manner which ensures they cannot fall into the wrong hands. So, if you have paperwork that is particularly sensitive, consider contacting one of the companies such as www.mustdestroy.com, which can confidentially dispose of your paperwork forever. Alternatively, many computer shops also sell personal shredders which can be used to shred paperwork. Saving a box for the 5 November bonfire is another option.

Don't look back! Once something has been allocated its rightful place either in the skip, the boot sale pile or for keeps, just move on to the next thing. It's much easier to convince yourself to keep something than it is to dispose of it.

In 2001 Christie's Football Memorabilia sale saw Danny Blanchflower's 1963 UEFA Cup Winner's Medal realise £10,575 having been lying unrecognised for eleven years in a claret jug the vendor had purchased at auction in Ealing for just £12.

Clutter or Cash?

Collectable items that are likely to have a value to someone, either at a boot sale, on eBay or at auction, are those in general that fulfil certain criteria. For those with no experience in this area and dealing with their first clear-out there can be an automatic fear that everything is 'collectable'. This is not the case, whatever you may hear at boot sales! For example, standard cheap plain drinking glasses are one of the hardest items to shift at a boot sale – they are quite literally ten a penny. However, coloured-glass drinking glasses, any featuring company names or brewery names such as Guinness, or those that are clearly of quality with a Wedgwood, Dartington, Caithness or Waterford name etched on, or that have any identifiable etched signature are likely to have a value. Items that were of poor quality in Edwardian times are still of poor quality today and if they are damaged they are virtually worthless. So look at every item in terms of:

Quality – does the item appear to be very well made, detailed and likely to have been quite expensive when it was made?

Usability – does the item have a practical function that it can still perform?

Age – does the piece seem to have age or could you still pick it up in Woolworths today?

> In 2002 Gorringes auction house in Sussex sold a silver Elizabethan communion cup for £5,300 which had been purchased at a car boot sale for £20.

Provenance – no one knows your family history in the way that you do. If you find items that could have a connection with a family member who was famous or infamous in any particular field and you can prove the provenance, the most ordinary item can suddenly rocket in value.

Era – it may not be to your personal taste but when you look at it does it scream 1970s disco fever, or 1950s kitchenalia, or 1930s Art Deco streamlined shape? If it clearly epitomises a particular moment in time then it is likely to have a value to someone.

Markings – always check pieces carefully for clues that will help you identify a piece and therefore give you information that will help you get started on valuing an item. These range from backstamps on the base of pottery and ceramic items, which most of the time include the details of the manufacturer, the designer and the name or range of the series from which the piece comes.

Craftsmanship – with furniture it's quite easy to spot a handmade piece from a machine-manufactured piece in the sense that carved wood will reveal the small chisel marks of the carpenter who worked on it, while manufactured items are more uniform and the joints are likely to be completely symmetrical and 'too perfect' to be handcrafted.

Design – is the item something that stands out as being different from other similar cups and saucers, chairs or books? It's possible that although there may be no markings as such a specialist can identify the piece as being designed by a particular respected and collected designer and therefore it has potential value.

Skip It or Sell It?

Just about everything in your home will fall into one of the categories below and by assessing each piece, allocating it a category and then using the checklist on the previous pages, you should have a fairly firm idea about whether something is worth getting properly valued or not.

PAPER

Old newspapers, family records, bills, photograph albums, old magazines and general paperwork is often referred to as ephemera if it has a collectable value. I have bought several photograph albums from boot sales simply because I think they offer wonderful snapshots of life gone by. One I purchased included a shot of the *Queen Mary* prior to her launch and I used this as inspiration to commission a Lorna Bailey Cruise Liner vase in a limited edition of 100 which sold out instantly when I launched it in 2003 to mark the launch of the *Queen Mary II*. There's something quite emotive and sad about seeing old

Inspired by the photograph I found at a boot sale of the *Queen Mary* pre-launch, I commissioned a liner vase in a limited edition of 100. It sold out instantly for £155.

photograph albums and other personal memories at boot sales. However, there are collectors for these, as after seventy-five years the photographer's copyright on an image expires so there are people who buy up such albums with a view to creating a library of shots that typify an era for use in publications.

In August 1999 Christie's sold some of the original sketches for the Kodak girl which were then used as part of the film company's advertising campaign. Found at a flea market in France, they realised £3,450.

BOOKS

Check whether or not a book is a first edition. If a book says, for example, 'first published in 1955' or 'third edition' it's unlikely to have considerable value unless it is signed by a famous author, is of considerable age or has great illustrations by the likes of Arthur Rackham. There is a market for books on sports of all kinds, cooking and famous figures. Harrington Books has a great website at www.peter-harrington-books.com and Dominic Winter Auctioneers are book-auction specialists.

There is a huge market for books, especially first editions and those with great illustrations.

TEXTILES

Carpets, rugs, cushions, curtains, tablecloths, scarves and basically anything that is made of material can have a value either to first-time buyers seeking to kit out their home at little cost or to interior designers. Look for identification of the material itself. I have purchased several pairs of Liberty of London printed William Morris design curtains, which can either be turned into cushion covers or used as they are for just £2 a pair – considerably less than the retail price. I also know someone who retrieved, with permission, a rug from a skip, which turned out to be an Islamic prayer rug that later sold at Bonhams for £5,000.

FURNITURE

Sofas and anything that clearly does not pass fire and safety regulations cannot be sold either by yourself at a boot sale or by charity shops. Large lumps of furniture from IKEA and other recent manufacturers are extremely cumbersome for boot sales but it's worth checking with local charity shops whether or not they would be interested in picking up your old furniture. Just remember to use your 'Clutter or Cash' checklist here, as I once bought a fabulous Arts and Crafts hall stand complete with inset metalwork and cabuchon for £100 from a charity shop.

In November 1998 Christie's realised £6,900 for a publicity brochure for first- and second-class passengers aboard the Titanic *and the* Olympic *– which had been found in the drawer of a bureau in a house in Somerset.*

GLASS

Damaged glass is dangerous and virtually impossible to repair so dispose of it carefully or, if it is suitable, at a local council-run bottle bank.

UTILITY

Anything that serves a practical purpose and is non-electrical, including stepladders, saucepans, cutlery, ironing boards, suitcases, mirrors, bathroom accessories, etc can all be of use to other people even if you have since replaced such items with newer examples. If something is wearing out, no longer used, has been usurped or is simply surplus to requirements – let's be honest, how many mugs does any house actually require – get rid of them. Anything that is part of a set but that set has long since been split up, does not match your current or planned replacement decor, must go and that usually includes the Pyrex dishes! Pictures may not be to your taste any more but picture framing can be an expensive exercise. I recently bought a large map of Cheshire from a boot sale for £30. It needed re-framing and the re-framing cost £100, so if the pictures are poor quality, simple mass-produced prints or clearly have no value under the 'Clutter or Cash' checklist, consider saving the frame alone if you like it as it may be possible to reuse it in future. Otherwise, just sell the picture itself at a boot sale but remember that even prints and posters can have a value. I once bought a large David Hockney 1988 Metropolitan Museum of Art exhibition framed poster from the Denham boot sale for £3 – it was worth £150– £200; and at the West Wycombe boot sale I bought a limited-edition Peter Scott framed print for £1 – it was worth about £45.

CHINA

Anything that has chips, cracks, old repairs, is missing its partner, e.g. a cup without a saucer, bears the words 'dishwasher and microwave proof', is transfer printed or 'made in China' is unlikely to have a great value, although complete sets of dining or kitchen items are saleable.

ELECTRICAL

Old microwaves, televisions, radios, deep fat fryers, alarm clocks, vacuum cleaners, music centres, wall and ceiling lights all need to be disposed of carefully. For fridges and freezers there are legal requirements about their proper disposal in order to protect the environment, and you can check how to dispose of these responsibly with your local council. In the case of items that still work properly, some charity shops will consider picking up such pieces and reselling them, but only if they are in good condition. Remember, if you do attempt to sell electrical items at a boot sale then you will need to remove all the plugs in order to conform with health and safety regulations. Given the number of unsold toasters, microwaves and deep fat fryers I have seen at boot sales, I would suggest that you save yourself the time and effort and simply dispose of them in the skip.

TOYS AND GAMES

Anything that is licensed or typifies an era has a value in this market and more modern toys are increasingly being sought after too. I purchased a set of three *Tots TV* large rag doll toys for £6 at the Clitheroe boot sale and they later sold on eBay for

£48. Although this particular model of toy may no longer be made, it's still extremely recent, having been available in the shops within the last five years. Some charity shops now refuse to take toys simply on the basis of space while others are considering opening specialist stores that concentrate on mother and baby/child items including toys, so check first. Board games have a value providing they are classics such as Colditz, On the Buses, Spitting Image or, more recently, Hero Quest. I've purchased Hero Quest board games for £1 which have sold for £35 on eBay. Any toys or games that are broken, incomplete or without their original boxes are unlikely to have a great value but mint and boxed examples of anything toy or game related will be easy to sell at boot sales.

A sweetbox containing its original unopened 1968 Beatles Yellow Submarine bubble gum packets sold on eBay for £15,100 in December 2002. Just forty bubblegum packs were contained in the box, so effectively each packet of thirty-four-year old gum cost £377.50.

CLOTHES

These should always be washed and ironed, whether they are going to a boot sale or a charity shop. Only the items that you know are heading to the dump should be bagged up, labelled and skipped. Bear in mind that branches of certain supermarkets have their own initiatives that can be supported here. For example, where I live the local Somerfield store has a permanent bin outside for old shoes, which are then sent out to Third World countries and this means that someone gets use from them.

PERSONAL

Old medicines, toiletries, make-up, deodorants, towels, etc should all be dumped responsibly. However, if bottles of perfume or medicine appear to fall into the 'Age' category of your 'Clutter or Cash' checklist, you should empty the contents and then check up the actual piece to see whether it is collectable or not.

A gentleman who bought an early English medicine bottle for £1 at a boot sale later sold it through BBR Auctions for £2,900.

HOBBIES AND SPORTS

If I had a pound for every running or rowing machine I have seen for sale at a boot sale I would be retired by now, similarly with golf clubs, tennis rackets and roller skates. Many people take up a hobby only to drop it after a certain time and much of this hobby equipment ends up at boot sales. It's a great place to purchase such items and test a hobby yourself to see whether you like it without laying out a lot of money. Large items of gym equipment is never likely to bring a great return compared to the hassle of transporting it to a boot sale or charity shop, so consider dumping it. Lighter items, such as golf clubs, usually sell quite well and there are boot sale dealers who concentrate on just selling these or bikes or other sports equipment, such as fishing rods and accessories. There is a huge market for antique and quality sports equipment and so if anything you have fits into the categories in the 'Clutter or Cash' section check it out.

In 1998 Sotheby's sold two hand-hammered Gutty golf balls, which had been found on a golf course, for £16,100.

Inside and Out

It's not just the interior of the home and the obvious places, such as the garage and the loft, that need to be cleared. What about the shed and the garden in general? In 2001 three *Bluebird* operation team overalls sold for £2,580 at Holloway's Auctioneers in Banbury, Oxford. They had been found abandoned in a garage in Kent and belonged to Ken Ritchie, who worked with Donald Campbell's chief engineer Leo Villa from 1954 on the *Bluebird* hydroplane K7, which was the one in which Campbell lost his life.

Sotheby's in Sussex has two sales a year featuring garden items from flower pots to statues and there are hundreds of dealers and companies specialising in reclamation – the retrieval of architectural items for resale. LASSCO in London, for example, once had a church font for sale that saw interest from a DJ who was considering using it for his decks and an American who was considering buying it to use as a springboard for his swimming pool. Old sinks, taps, greenhouses, gardening, carpentry and plumbing tools are all sought after, as are beehives, builder's scales, watering cans and garden gnomes – if they have some age to them. Here are some examples of items that have been discovered in the most unusual places after being overlooked by their owners for years:

An ancient stone carving used as a headstone for a pet cat made £201,600 at Sotheby's in London in 2004. The vendor's husband was a stonemason and had found the slab in a quarry years previously. In fact, the 18 x 17-inch sculpture depicted a half-length figure of St Peter and was thought to be from King Alfred's reign, AD 871–891.

In April 2002 Christie's Islamic Art and Manuscripts sale saw a medieval door realise £766,850 – it was about to be made into a coffee table before William Robinson, Christie's Islamic Art specialist, spotted it during a routine valuation.

Lord Pearce, a judge, bought a statue by Adrien de Vries called Dancing Faun in 1951 as part of a garden job lot. He paid 7 guineas, equivalent to £7.35 today. Sotheby's sold the statue in 1989 for £6m and it is now at the Getty Foundation.

In Yorkshire, Alan Blakeman, who owns British Bottle Review, a magazine and auction house specialising in bottles, is used to amazing finds turning up. 'Recently we had a gentleman phone us who had bought a book on collectables for £1 at a car boot sale. In the book, he spotted a rare cobalt blue coffin poison bottle and recognised it as being the same as one his brother had dug up some twenty years previously from a dump site in Pontefract. The bottle is extremely rare and is one of only five known examples. It was placed into auction and we sold it for just under £10,000. Another boot sale find was a Hamilton bottle purchased for £1 and then sold for £1,000.'

A gentleman who bought an old car to run around in, decided to renovate the vehicle and found a metal plate had been used to fill a gaping hole on the car floor. The plate turned out to be an enamel sign advertising Matchless Metal Polish and it was sold for £700 – more than he had paid for the car originally.

A thirteenth-century ring which was found by a Norfolk housewife in her back garden was sold at Bonhams six years ago for £4,140.

In 2002 The Fate of Persephone *by the Arts and Crafts artist Walter Crane was sold at Christie's for £424,650, setting a new world record for the artist at auction. The painting was rediscovered by a ten-year-old old American boy who was convinced that the work of art hanging in his school library was indeed a lost Walter Crane painting and pieced together the provenance that proved this to be the case.*

In March 2002 Bearne's Auctioneers in Exeter sold an English porcelain miniature milk pail produced by Lunds of Bristol in around 1750 measuring just 7cm wide. One of only six known examples it made £18,500, having been spotted during a routine insurance valuation at a Devon property.

In 2002 Hall's Auctioneers sold a tin-glazed earthenware cat dating from 1677 for £45,000 after it was discovered hidden behind a £20 Royal Crown Derby saucer which had been more treasured by the vendor than the cat figurine.

A woman was reunited with her twenty-two-year-old wedding dress after finding it on the rails of her local charity shop. Gillian Hodge from Heathfield in East Sussex had sold the full-length white gown fourteen years earlier. The dress, still

with the lucky threepenny bit sewn into the label, was reunited
with its original owner for the sum of £45.

Conclusion

Don't rush your clutter clear-out or it could cost you a fortune.

In February 2005, for example, a thirty-five-year-old woman snapped up an 18-inch charger plate at a Manchester boot sale for £1, with a hunch that it might be valuable. Her instincts were confirmed when another boot-seller immediately offered her £100 for the piece. It is in fact a Clarice Cliff 'Age of Jazz' charger in the 'Latona Dahlia' pattern, which originally cost 10 shillings in 1933. It sold at Christie's auction house in London (Sunday 20 February 2005) for £1,976 against an estimate of £1,500.

We must feel sorry for the poor stallholder innocently cashing in his clutter, only to later read about his £1 plate in every national newspaper. A simple Internet search for Clarice Cliff or a check on eBay would have given the seller some indication of its potential value.

Whatever you do and however much you want to clear those crammed rooms, bear in mind the saying 'more haste, less speed' and remember that it's always better to be safe than sorry. If you're taking the time to clear out your clutter, take the time to check all your items – not carrying out a thorough check could quite literally cost you a £2,000 cheque.

CHAPTER TWO

WHAT IS COLLECTABLE?

There was a time when antiques ruled the world of collecting. Today it's the modern collectables and limited editions that dominate. Just as the City opened up to the Essex barrow boys in the 1980s, so the world of collecting opened up to all with the release of figurines, books and toys which were produced in sets and limited numbers.

It's an astute form of marketing that works on the old economic rules of supply and demand. Providing demand outstrips supply the price of the product should rise. I can remember learning that in my very first economics lesson and it's something that manufacturers have very much taken on board.

In 1998, at a collectors' fair, I launched a limited edition commissioned from Royal Doulton. Part of the Winnie the Pooh licensed series, 'Wol Signs the Rissolution' was the first single figure to be released in a limited edition of just 2,500. Demand was excessive from collectors for this piece and it quickly sold

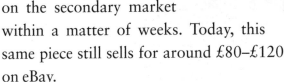

I commissioned Royal Doulton to make 'Wol Signs the Rissolution' in 1998 – a limited edition of 2,500 costing £39.95. It sold out and now sells for £80–£120 on eBay.

out at its £39.95 retail price and hit the dizzy heights of £200 a piece on the secondary market within a matter of weeks. Today, this same piece still sells for around £80–£120 on eBay.

So what was the secret? Well, simple really. At this time the collectors' market reached frenzied peaks of demand. People were using it as a form of investment, rather than actually buying the pieces because they liked them. Most people would buy two examples, one to keep and one to sell on. As a result, limited editions such as Wol sold out twice as quickly with those who missed the boat able to buy only through the secondary market at antiques and collectors' fairs or through the Internet. Following those basic economic rules, as demand outstripped supply, up went the price.

In 1999, to mark the eclipse, I commissioned Lorna Bailey to make a series of four chargers (large wall plaques). The first, to mark the eclipse, cost £155 and sold out in a day and within a month one had been sold at an antiques fair for £350. The key, of course, is knowing when to buy and when to sell. Someone who bought the eclipse charger when it came out more than doubled their money within a month by selling the piece very quickly to catch a collector prepared to pay top money to secure an example for his or her collection. Since that time, the eclipse charger has sold on eBay for between £180 and £290.

It would seem that a quick turnaround is the key. If you want to make money, you need to have your finger on the pulse of what limited editions are being launched, when and at what price and be prepared to sell the item on just as quickly. There's always a burst of excitement as a limited edition sells out. The word quickly spreads that demand was so high, the edition expired within a day and this very often means the limited edition becomes a legend in its own lifetime. Yet waiting until the excitement has abated can be costly, as the price almost always falls back considerably. A good limited edition will always make a profit over the longer term, in the case of both Wol and the charger it would be impossible to have invested the purchase price in a bank account and have achieved a return comparable to the selling price these pieces realise today.

But the old auction adage comes in here too – buyer beware! If it was all so easy and so simple why would any of us go to work? Surely, we could just sit at home looking out for limited editions, buy them and then sell them on for a profit. Well, for every great limited edition that provides a profit the collectors' market is scattered with examples that have fallen by the wayside.

There are many reasons why a limited edition may or may not work but the key to success is to learn as much as possible about the pitfalls in order to avoid them!

Limited by Number

Numbered limited editions are always favoured by collectors, particularly those that are clearly stamped on the base of a piece. The manufacturer Wade Ceramics has produced figures limited by numbers for many years. It issues certificates with each limited edition to show what number the piece is within the edition size, e.g. Number 5 of a limited edition of 500. Royal Doulton always scored the underside of each piece from a limited edition with both the number of the piece and the size of the edition. The Royal Doulton route is of course the more favoured among collectors, as there is little chance of faking the numbers. The problem with issuing certificates but not adding the information to the base of a piece is that, thanks to modern technology, unscrupulous people can start copying certificates. By default, many manufacturers find it impossible to issue absolute precise numbers.

There is usually a 10% overproduction on any limited edition. This means that some surplus is produced, which should of course be destroyed in order to ensure that the overall edition size is correct. Manufacturers have always understood this and have taken steps to ensure that surpluses are destroyed but, as is human nature, on occasion temptation can prove too much and surpluses 'walk' and become available on the open market, together with faked or fraudulent certificates.

Given that the collectors' market is all about confidence in a product or limited edition, this can be lethal for an entire limited edition run. In 1997, in conjunction with C&S Collectables the specialists in Betty Boop figures in this country, I issued a limited edition of 500 Wade Ceramics Betty Boop wall plaques. The 500 made for me were in a red colour with a further 1,250 taken from the same mould made in white for C&S. They sold out instantly at £65 each and were sent out with the correct limited edition certificates. Nevertheless, because of firing faults and the demands in terms of production of making

500, a separate box of further pieces was supplied. Under the contract terms this was perfectly acceptable – overproduction was always a possibility. However, what was vital to the market was the fact that these were then destroyed – quite literally smashed to pieces so that they could never get onto the collectors' market with fake certificates and be passed off as part of the original 500. Unfortunately, not every dealer is as reputable and honourable as C&S and not every manufacturer as honest as Wade Ceramics. It's easy to see how this oversupply loophole could be exploited.

There is plenty that collectors can do to ensure they are buying correctly and not falling into the trap of purchasing pieces that are not all they seem. And just as with stocks and shares in the City, this involves doing your homework and sharing information.

First port of call should be finding out as much as possible about the company or individual behind any one limited edition. Arguably, the King of Collectables is a gentleman called Nick Tzimas, who for many years ran UKI Ceramics and had a contract with Royal Doulton to produce numbered limited editions of the Bunnykins figurines range. At one time there were waiting lists, years long, from collectors desperate to be offered the chance to buy a limited-edition Bunnykin at the issue price direct from UKI Ceramics, rather than having to buy them from auctions or dealers at a considerably higher price. When UKI Ceramics issued 'Trick or Treat' Bunnykins in 1995 it was a limited edition of 1,500 and sold for £45, but within a couple of years it was selling for £450 at auctions and antiques fairs. The very fact that demand was so high meant that the price on the collectors' or secondary market rose rapidly and usually maintained its peak price. Nick Tzimas became a legend in his own lifetime for his ability to commission and market this particular range and so confidence in the Bunnykins market alone grew and grew. As more collectors learnt about the company and its success, more and more people wanted a slice of the action and so the demand for each limited edition rose. This was a company whose products collectors could happily purchase, confident of a great return.

Auctions have a great role too in this area. Even Bonhams in London took notice and in the bastions of its great New Bond Street address, hundreds of little Bunnykins figures would be viewed pre-sale by collectors keen to snap up an example. The very fact that an auction house as grand as Bonhams took notice further increased confidence. At the same time Potteries Spe-

UKI Ceramics issued this figure in 1995 for £45 and within a couple of years it was changing hands for £450.

cialist Auctions in Stoke-on-Trent carved out a name for itself as the place to purchase other limited editions by manufacturers such as Lorna Bailey and Wade Ceramics – companies whose limited editions provided good returns but didn't reach the dizzy heights needed for Bonhams to pay attention. Keeping a check on auction catalogues and the prices realised means that collectors have an instant reference guide for the limited edition, the actual piece, the edition number and the price collectors are prepared to pay. Obviously, the arrival of eBay has adjusted the market somewhat. At one time, the only way of getting your hands on a limited-edition Bunnykins figure was to be on the UKI Ceramics mail-order list, attend a UKI fair or be friends with a dealer who could get you an example even though you'd instantly be paying a premium on the retail price. Alternatively you had to buy at a traditional auction. Clearly, while Bonhams and Potteries Specialist Auctions had identified and capitalised on this new collectables market, many traditional regional auction houses were simply bemused by the whole modern limited-edition market and would reject any attempts by collectors to sell such modern pieces through their houses. As a result, options to buy were limited – until eBay really caught on of course. Suddenly, by simply going online collectors could just sit and wait and bid on any Bunnykins piece listed if they were prepared to pay the price. Any limited edition, however rare, will eventually surface on eBay. If it is particularly sought after and sells for a high price the word spreads quickly and other collectors keen to realise a profit will start listing their identical pieces from the same edition. The fact that supply starts to catch up with demand means that the hammer price starts to recede. Suddenly, a collector in Japan sees that the Bunnykins Halloween 'Trick or Treat' piece can fetch £300 on eBay and opts to list his item, as does a collector in Australia and another in Britain. From nowhere there are now three identical examples available and possibly only two people actually looking for that piece and so the demand undermines the number of examples on offer and down comes the price.

The true eBay effect on the market started to be felt as the Internet boom took off in 1999 and for every example of an item selling for way, way above the expected price on eBay there were plenty of pieces which failed to realise their basic reserve price. Perhaps it's telling that, today, Royal Doulton makes its Bunnykins figures in the Far East, Nick Tzimas no longer commissions the vast range of Bunnykins figurines he once did, and Bonhams in New Bond Street no longer hosts auctions dedicated to the little Bunnies made post-1972.

Arguably another problem facing the booming and now declining Bunnykins market was over-information. At one stage just about every collector of anything had heard or knew of the boom in Bunnykins. The success of ebay.com meant that this information was there for everyone to see and learn from – millions of instant experts were born and woe betide the collector who didn't understand or keep an eye on the prices each Bunnykin realised on eBay.

But the frenzy over the Bunnykins market provided opportunities for collectors clever enough to realise that if this was happening in one market there must be opportunities elsewhere. One of the greatest attributes found in the modern limited-editions market is the fact that most collectors, whether British, English, Welsh, Scottish, American, Japanese, Swedish or German, like British limited editions to be made in Britain. It's a fact that British manufacturers themselves have understood and capitalised on by making sure their editions are British-made – until more recently, of course, in the case of Royal Doulton, where economic demands and financial concerns forced the company to shift most production of such collectables overseas.

Companies such as Merrythought and Dean's the teddy bear manufacturers have been astute at marketing themselves on the basis that they are still designing and making their products in Britain. Collectors were quick to understand that British-made limited editions did well and an example of a market that has come into its own thanks to eBay has to be Border Fine Arts (BFA).

This company, based in Cumbria, has for many years been producing naturalistic resin models of animals, birds and more recently complete tableaux of farming scenes. One of its most successful modellers is Ray Ayres, whose pieces for BFA were all issued with the distinctive Ray Ayres signature and numbered individually in the cases of limited editions. The ranges proved especially popular with those in rural areas and farmers in particular, who clearly admired the depictions of old Ford tractors ploughing up the fields. These pieces were never cheap when sold. Tableaux could cost £250–£400 back in 1997 and individual mice on fruit – a really sought-after range among collectors – could be £60–£80 a piece. So while the range was considerably upmarket compared with ceramic collectables such as Bunnykins, many ignored BFA at their peril. The arrival of eBay made many collectors suddenly sit up and take notice. Certain pieces realised the most amazing prices. Martin Donovan, collectables specialist, who buys and sells on eBay, explains:

By taking a good look at what was selling on ebay.com, I realised just what demand there was for BFA pieces and made a point of looking for these at boot sales. I also invested in a proper collector's guide on the subject that meant I had a photographic reference for each and every piece. After a while you do get to recognise particular styles and the feel of the BFA products but initially I was really lucky. In just one year by trawling boot sales I bought a pair of badgers playing at a boot sale for £5 which sold for £350 on ebay.com, a border terrier chasing a hedgehog for £3 which made £350 and a mouse next to a candle for £2.49 which sold for £210. It's something I would never have particularly looked out for until I came across the pieces on eBay and realised what they made. It's vital of course that all the pieces I've found are truly Border Fine Arts and sought-after Ray Ayres pieces. There are a lot of similar-looking resin figures, but if they are not BFA, forget it! I know of another friend for example who purchased a large kestrel piece at a boot sale for £5. It was damaged but at this time BFA offered a repair service for broken pieces so my friend sent this off, got it repaired and sold it on ebay.com for £1,000.

Limited by 'Time'

In 2002, under contract with the Victoria and Albert Museum, I commissioned a Lorna Bailey 'Orb' vase to mark the museum's Art Deco exhibition. The constraints of working with an institution and planning with a manufacturer made it impossible to actually issue a fixed limited edition and so I opted for a piece that would be made for just six months, until the exhibition ended. Any orders taken during this time would be honoured, after which no further examples would be made. In all, 70 examples were made, selling for £155 each. In fact, this turned out to be an incredibly low edition size – particularly in light of the fixed editions, such as the eclipse charger, which was a limited edition of 100. Clearly, for collectors there are times when 'limited by time' can mean that the overall edition size is a lot smaller and this would, by the laws of supply and demand, mean

The Lorna Bailey 'Orb' vase commissioned to mark the Victoria and Albert Museum's Art Deco exhibition in 2003. It retailed at £155 and was time limited; only 70 were eventually produced, which is less than a normal limited-edition commission.

the price rises dramatically. While the 'Orb' vase regularly sells for £200+ it's clear that collectors do prefer to know exactly where they stand and what the overall edition size is before they buy.

Perhaps one of the most successful 'time limited' editions was the set of Winnie the Pooh figures released in 1996 to mark the centenary of the famous A.A. Milne bear. The charming selection consisted of twelve figurines and for this year alone were made bearing a special gold backstamp indicating that it was a centenary set. There was no commitment or requirement to buy every single piece, i.e. the complete set, but many collectors made a point of ordering the entire range with the special backstamp through their Royal Doulton outlets. Once the year had passed, Royal Doulton continued to make the individual figurines but not with the special backstamp in gold. As a result, a set of those figures which cost £150 in 1996 now makes £350+ on eBay.

Discontinued and Discounted

There's nothing that helps a market or the price of a collectable more than the word 'discontinued'. This effectively means that, for whatever reason, the model or piece is no longer in production. The shorter the production run has been the better the effect on demand and because the piece is no longer generally available, i.e. there's a lack of ready supply, the price rises. This has been seen on many occasions through the years, particularly with the Royal Doulton ranges of Bunnykins, Beatrix Potter, Beswick and Royal Albert pieces and their more traditional figurines.

While UKI Ceramics were producing limited-edition Bunny-kins, Royal Doulton supplied the retail trade with endless examples available generally. These were, until recently, neither time limited nor limited by number – they were simply, after a certain time, 'discontinued' and no longer produced, usually being replaced by new models.

Conveniently, most manufacturers are keen to issue their collectors' clubs and websites with details of the forthcoming discontinuations. This makes sense, as it gives collectors the chance to purchase the items that are going out of production before they are available only on the secondary market. Of course, the more cynical might argue that this can also result in an increase in demand for certain items that are to be discontinued, thus boosting sales for the retail trade and manufacturers. Either way, it can work to both parties' advantage.

Royal Doulton launched its own Halloween Bunnykins figure, a Bunnykins figure popping out of a pumpkin, in 1993 and by the time it was discontinued in 1997 it was selling in shops for £17. One of my favourite Bunnykins pieces, simply because it's fun and witty, the Halloween Bunnykins quickly rose to £25–£35 on the secondary market after it was discontinued.

Such was the success of 'discontinued' collectables that Royal Doulton became known for its 'Drop Dead' policy – the issuing of edicts listing whole ranges of items that were to be 'discontinued' with immediate effect. Collectors would wait eagerly for these lists to be issued, knowing that whatever was on them would, by the time the information was released, already be no longer in production at the company's Stoke-on-Trent factory. As a result, the only way to buy the pieces would be to trawl the retail shops for examples left sitting on the shelves.

This 'Drop Dead' policy was complemented by the 'Last Chance to Buy' (LCB) opportunities. The LCB information would list all the ranges that were to be discontinued but in a few months' time, thus giving collectors their last chance to buy. The LCB policy was never as successful as the 'Drop Dead' announcements, for the simple reason that there was no need to rush out there and get the pieces because you knew exactly when the deadline for the production range was and could take your time tracking them down. Many shrewd dealers, of course, invested thousands in sweeping across the country purchasing 'Drop Dead' and LCB items. I know of many cases where dealers simply bought up all the examples they could find and stored them away, waited until the price rose on the secondary market and then quietly sold them through auction houses around the country, on eBay and at antique fairs and boot sales. It doesn't take much to work out that if you bought 100 Halloween Bunnykins at £17 – an overall investment of £1,700 and then sold each one for £25, i.e. a £8 profit, you would have made £800.

There are many examples of even greater profits to be had. For example, when Royal Doulton discontinued its Snowman range of figurines, made under official licence to the famous illustrated story, in 1994 they were selling in the shops for £15 a figure. Overall there were twenty in the series and one collector I met shortly after filming *Boot Sale Challenge* in 1999 had purchased the entire range. Paul Foster, of Southend-on-Sea in Essex and a keen boot-saler explains:

> I just liked the figures and had bought each one from the shops. When I knew the range was going to end, I started picking up doubles at a discount. Most of the shops, includ-

ing Debenhams and Keddies, an old family-run department store which has since closed, were selling the figures and the tableware, such as wall plates and mugs, at between 25% and 50% off so I thought it was a good idea to get extras in case I ever broke any.

Little did Paul know at the time that this entire range would stand the test of time. Given that the pieces were made when Royal Doulton was producing its figures in Stoke-on-Trent, as opposed to the Far East as is the case today, and that they were of such a classic and popular Christmas children's story, demand continued long after the range was discontinued. It wasn't long before Bonhams in London was selling 'Skier' Snowman, generally accepted to be the hardest to find, for £800+. By 2002, Paul had decided to part with his complete collection and realised £2,000 for the full set of twenty figures, which cost just £300 to buy from 1985 when first issued, a return on his investment that not even the housing market can match – even I managed to find 'Cowboy' Snowman at a boot sale for £8 and sell it on eBay for £85!

It's not uncommon for items that are being discontinued to then also be discounted. The manufacturers, keen to clear 'dead' or old stock, will allow the retailers to clear their shelves ready for new products by selling the old pieces at a discount. When I first moved to back to my hometown there was a shop called TableTalk, which had been going for years. I can remember buying Wade Whimsies

Royal Doulton 'Skier' Snowman is the hardest to find in the range of 20 figures produced. They originally sold at £800+ each, but prices have since fallen and now it sells for £350–£400.

for friends' birthdays from this shop at 25p each when I was at the local junior school some thirty years ago! More importantly, once I could buy collectables this shop was a regular place to visit on a weekly basis. I have often thought what a great thing hindsight is and how much I would have bought, at a discount, if only I had known how prices would rocket on the secondary market! I can remember seeing Border Fine Arts tableaux with 25% off taking the price down to £250, which now make £1,000+. Nevertheless, I managed to get plenty of bargains.

Border Fine Arts also had the Brambly Hedge licence for a number of years and produced resin figurines from the various Jill Barklem stories before the licence ran out and the first range was discontinued in 1997. I should add that BFA still makes Brambly Hedge ranges today, but these are not as sought after as the very first range issued. TableTalk in Upminster had several pieces discontinued and I purchased the Winter Fireplace at £3.75 – 75% off the original retail price. I sold it in 2002 for £85 on eBay.

Licensed Limited Editions

The success of a limited edition and its price on the secondary market is very often dictated in part by the terms of a licence. The most successful figures or figurines, toys or teddies tend to be the ones that reflect a classic, well-known character. These character licences range from Brambly Hedge and the Snowman to Peter Pan, where the rights were left by J.M. Barrie to Great Ormond Street Hospital, and Winnie the Pooh where the rights left by A.A. Milne to his club was one of the most expensive licence rights ever purchased by Disney some years ago. The very fact that Winnie the Pooh outsells Mickey Mouse in the Disney stores goes some way to showing what a commercial success a licensed character can be.

While Royal Doulton capitalised on its success with licences by issuing Disney characters, Snowman, Brambly Hedge and Beatrix Potter characters for years under licence, Coalport had never been able to replicate the success of such licensed products until it took up with a very disorientated bear found at Paddington Station. Its licensed Paddington Bear figures were first produced in 1976 and cost around £10–£15 each. The company has since issued new versions under licence but the original Coalport ceramic set consisted of 42 figures and when they were discontinued between 1988 and 2001 they quickly rose in value on the secondary market. Today, a Paddington 'Magician with Rabbit' can realise as much as £185.

I have plenty of experience working with and under licence. Applying for licences is a long and arduous process of liaison with both the artists themselves, assuming they are still alive, or their representatives through the licensing companies, which applies whether the artist is alive or dead! An up-front payment is almost always required and calculated on forecast sales of each individual product or piece; the licensing company have to approve every stage of the concept, from the initial drawings to ensure that the character is being depicted in the way the artist intended, through to the approval of initial prototypes – the first time the modeller has actually modelled the piece. Only when everything from the model's shape to the colour of paint used, the backstamp each piece will bear and the way the item will be marketed has been approved can the actual launch go ahead.

By default this can mean up to two years from the start of the process to the actual launch of the first pieces in a range. Then, on top of the initial investment made, the licensing company is entitled to a percentage of each sale. Often this commitment has to be made and is enforceable regardless of how successful the range becomes.

While the Beatrix Potter licence enabled Royal Doulton's Beswick and Royal Albert brands to make figurines from the stories' pieces for nearly 100 years, bringing in plenty of money, the company's decision to invest in the Harry Potter licence did not have the same magic effect. I attended the launch of the Harry Potter range in 1999 at the company's Stoke-on-Trent headquarters and there was not a single piece on display. By the time the items finally arrived on the shelves in the shops, the huge marketing wave from the first film, *Harry Potter and the Philosopher's Stone*, had passed. Indeed, the range was so extensive that most collectors were simply confused. The fact that the range had also been made overseas rather than within the Stoke-on-Trent factories, to save time and money, increased collectors' resistance and it wasn't long before Royal Doulton faced a huge loss on its investment and had issued 'Drop Dead' and LCB edicts on the initial ranges.

Annual and Celebration Limited Editions

Certain events happen every year without fail! Christmas, Easter, St Patrick's Day, St David's Day, St Andrew's Day, St

George's Day, Valentine's Day and Mother's Day to name but a few. Ever aware of a marketing opportunity, companies are extremely clever at tapping into the sentimental charm of these events. Virtually every year, various companies from Merrythought to Royal Doulton, Swatch to Lulu Guinness and Jean Paul Gaultier launch Christmas 'limited editions'. These are limited in time and event rather than by number, although admittedly Swatch does number its watches but these tend to be in the tens of thousands. These companies issue collectable products aimed at capitalising on the festive season for that particular year. Rather than restricting the numbers, they restrict the supply by making sure most examples launched bear the year. As a result the following year they can bring out another example and so on and so forth.

Swatch, the Swiss fashion watch manufacturer, is a past master at the marketing of its Christmas collectable watches, which usually command an instant premium among collectors. Its Christmas specials are eagerly awaited by Swatch Club members at home and abroad who frequently queue overnight outside Swatch stores ahead of the watches' arrival in order to secure an example. When I first started my weekly column in the *Financial Mail on Sunday* back in 1996, I tipped as a future Christmas collectable the Swatch Christmas Special X.I.A.N designed by Christian Lacroix, which retailed at £55 and four years later was selling for £220–£250. By 2000, Swatch's Christmas special 'World Party' in a worldwide limited edition of 2000 had collectors queuing overnight at retail outlets and Swatch shops to secure an example.

Royal Doulton issued its Santa Bunnykins 'Happy Christmas' from 1981, until discontinued in 1996, at a cost of £15, but in 1987 a few examples were made with a hole in one ear so it could be hung as an ornament on a Christmas tree. Available only in the USA, an example found at a boot sale in 2000 went on to make more than £1,000 at auction.

Christmas 'Surprise Bunnykins' retired at the end of 2000 having been produced since 1994 and by the time it was 'discontinued' it was retailing in shops at £17.85.

Hats off to Ty when it comes to making the most of an event. The launch of the legendary Ty Beanie Babies was in part

fuelled by Ty Warner's ability to bring out a different Beanie Baby Bear for every single Easter, Christmas, Halloween, Mother's Day, St Patrick's Day, St Andrew's Day, etc every single year. Disney stores quickly achieved the same with its combined Winnie the Pooh, Eeyore, Piglet and Tigger individual mini beanbag characters, issued every single holiday in a different costume and bearing the year embroidered somewhere about the characters' body

Ty knew how to make a market producing Beanie Babies for every occasion in every shape, form and size.

parts! The cost for collectors of chasing this annual Holy Grail is horrendous. In 1999 Disney's 'Christmas Tree Tigger' cost £6.99 and was in exceptionally short supply, which saw the price rise among collectors to £65 virtually overnight as they fought to secure an example. Just two years later, the Disney store was releasing no fewer than eighteen different variations of Winnie the Pooh and Mickey Mouse for the Christmas season, costing a total of £127 for collectors trying to chase and buy the lot. At this time, there was still a good chance that they would reach £10 each on the secondary market, thus realising £180 and a £53 profit. However, over the last three years I've seen enough Disney mini beanbag Christmas specials at boot sales being virtually given away to see that these have now regained their status as toys rather than collectables.

As if Christmas isn't enough, many collectors had to go through the millennium, which was forecast to bring chaos across the board and certainly did for collectors! Many manufacturers liaising with the Millennium Board so that they could feature the 'Millennium Man' logo found themselves swamped with paperwork and increasingly pushing the millennium deadline. Some still did not have product available by the end of 2000. However, once again, those with deep pockets ensured that Border Fine Arts' 'Threshing Machine' tableau of quite enormous proportions sold out despite its £1,500 retail price – by 2001 an example had sold at a specialist Border Fine Arts auction for £4,200.

Protoypes

These are arguably the most limited of all limited editions. A prototype is the first piece from which all others are made – the 'Adam' of the manufacturer's foray into a new collectable range. The prototype will be marked up as such on the base and will be the piece that is used as the approved and final example from which all others in the edition range will be copied. It will be the one that is kept by manufacturers to ensure that there is always an example in their archives as a reference. Until very recently this is exactly where the prototypes remained – in the archives and museums of manufacturers. However, with the millennium this all changed.

Royal Doulton's financial woes saw it announce the sale of both its Royal Doulton and Minton archives, which include thousands of prototype figures among other items from vases to tableware. The sales were conducted through Bonhams in London and some smaller items were released to Louis Taylor Auctioneers in Stoke-on-Trent. The most sought-after were of course the prototypes of models that were never, ever released – yet even prototypes for models that had been in production for years made ten times the retail price of their offspring.

The first of the Royal Doulton archive sales was held in 2001 and, including the Minton archives, ran until 2004 although items from the archives are still popping up from time to time in various sections of various Bonhams catalogues. The blow for collectors in Britain was that, because these items were sold by the manufacturer, VAT at 17.5% was payable on top of the commission price (the commission price itself incurs VAT so there was in fact a double VAT whammy). Only collectors from abroad could reclaim the VAT and as a result any British collectors buying from these sales found themselves paying virtually 30% on top of the price they thought they were due to pay.

Clearly, such a sale is unrepeatable and offered some wonderful examples of figures from Royal Doulton's heyday of manufacturing when design, not accountancy, ruled. However, whether any of these prototypes can actually achieve a profit remains to be seen. Most were sold to dedicated Royal Doulton collectors around the world and have yet to re-emerge onto the market. Some of the plainest, poorest models made six-figure sums and achieving these heights again will be tough.

Nevertheless, many other manufacturers realise that just the word prototype can be enough to achieve a premium. Many will donate prototypes to charity auctions or collectors' club events. But this has got to the point where most collectors find it simply confusing. There is also a feeling that there have been several cases where prototypes have popped up that have been simply labelled prototypes rather than actually being the original prototype models. Certainly some manufacturers will have more than one prototype if the model has had to be altered for whatever reason – but too many prototypes can certainly spoil the collectability of a piece.

Variations

Colour variations and model variations are others form of limited edition. Royal Doulton's original Beatrix Potter range, produced bearing a gold Beswick backstamp, remains a sought-after modern collectable range that has won collectors' hearts on the basis that there are so many variations. Some of these, such as the Royal Doulton lady figurine 'Top of the Hill', has seven model numbers and is known to come in at least fifty colour variations. Another example is Beswick's Beatrix Potter figure 'Tommy Brock' which has four variations to the actual model. These cases arose because it was discovered during manufacture that the item broke too easily, due to one part or another being too prominent. The model was altered to alleviate the problem and collectors immediately picked up on the fact that there was now a variation in the mix – naturally it's the former version rather than the latter that is then sought after.

Once again, Ty Warner's Beanie Baby ranges took this to ridiculous marketing extremes. By altering – slightly – the hang tags and tush tags that identify the individual Beanie Baby, collectors across the world went on a rummage searching for every single variation that might exist. Yet it can become such a full-time job that it backfires and collectors simply resist the search and turn their attention to other collectables.

In 2001 I launched the first of the new Adam Binder range with this particular artist and produced a limited edition of 500 'Kiss 'n' Tail' cat models made of resin. Within this edition there were ten made featuring blue flowers and ten with lilac flowers, whereas the rest of the edition had simple coloured leaves. Priced at £49.95, the edition itself sold out instantly and the general range quickly fetched £500+ on eBay while the variations realised up to and above £1,000 on eBay.

Collectors' Club Limited Editions

In March 2001 Moorcroft in Stoke-on-Trent launched its first 'Spring Weekend' event at which several products from its design studio were launched. On offer were 200 'Jonquilla' vases designed by Rachel Bishop and costing £345, which sold out to collectors on the day. True, these were limited editions numbered on the base and designed by one of the country's foremost design talents, but the point is that you could get your hands on one only if you were a member of the Moorcroft Collectors' Club had paid your annual dues and turned up on the day. This same piece now makes £800+ on eBay. At the same event a set of six boxed eggcups designed by other artists from within the design studio were sold for £185 – these were not limited editions as such but were available only up to April that year. By May this same set was selling for a 54% profit.

Moorcroft has the advantage of being steeped in history as a ceramic manufacturer. It was a forefront manufacturer in the Arts and Crafts movement in the early 1900s, with examples selling at Liberty in London, but nevertheless until recently it has maintained the ability to juggle good design and products with a high retail price and still provide a strong profit for collectors.

By 2002, I had commissioned a Moorcroft Bullerswood vase, which was designed by Rachel Bishop. Based on a recently discovered William Morris carpet found in Australia, the pot was momentous and stunning – I can say this as a credit to Rachel who provided the fabulous design. The limited edition of just 100 sold out at the Moorcroft Collectors' Club event in the autumn at £895. Just a year later, it was making £2,000+ on eBay and by October 2004 an example had sold at another Moorcroft Collectors' Club event for more than £8,000.

Every manufacturer has its own collectors' club, which is really nothing more than a glorified mailing list, except that collectors get the latest information about the companies'

Inspired by William Morris's 'Bullerswood' carpet, I commissioned a limited edition of 100 vases designed by Rachel Bishop. They originally retailed at £895 but recently one sold at a Moorcroft Collectors' Club event for £8,000.

products and opportunities to buy items exclusively available to collectors. This often means that some collectors miss out and are therefore desperate to get hold of examples even if this is on the secondary market and at a premium price.

Tips

Check eBay for the success of past Christmas or special day editions – what are they making? Why are some selling for more than others?

Check manufacturers' websites for new releases and proposed pieces that are to be launched with any special theme.

Find your local stockist of these manufacturers' products and ask to go on a waiting or mailing list so you are kept informed. Many retailers offer 10% discounts to regular buyers for their loyalty if they prove they will make return purchases from the same store.

Consider switching your credit card if you currently pay interest to one of the many '0% Interest-Free' companies offering credit cards – this will allow you to buy the collectable and give you a deadline for reselling it – hopefully at a profit and before the interest-free term expires.

Don't get carried away or 'fall in love' with the pieces if you are buying them to sell on. Never mix business with pleasure – if you are buying to sell at a profit, make sure that you do not get sentimentally attached to any one piece.

Make sure when you purchase a piece that you get the correct original box. Retailers frequently carry so much stock, and many manufacturers' boxes are so similar, that it is easy to get home and find that you have the wrong box for the piece and that will affect saleability. Obviously make sure that the box is in good condition and complete with any certificates.

If you get the opportunity to take any items to a manufacturer's or retailer's 'Event Day' where it can be signed by the artist that modelled the piece, do – it can add 5–15% to the resale price just having the artist's signature at the bottom of the piece.

Make sure you keep the original receipts both for your own records (for tax purposes when calculating your profit and what may be due to the taxman) but also as a record of how successful you are being at trading. Of course, should the worst happen, it also helps insurance claims to have the original purchase receipt.

Be prepared to take a loss. Yes it's very likely that over time some editions will do better than others – if you have too much capital invested and not enough sales going through you will end up in a rut, desperately unable to buy new stock and with all your money tied up in items that are not selling. Cut your losses. We've all had to do it. Learn from the experience, and assess what went wrong. Losses can be offset against profits for tax purposes, but they will also help you to release the money you have invested (albeit slightly less than you spent as you've not made the profits you hoped for) so that you can start again.

Limited editions or annual editions launched every year or as part of a range often see the first example command a premium. Make sure you get in at the start of any new launch. For example, Millennium Collectables launched its successful range of Royal Doulton manufactured advertising characters back in 2000 with the 'Golly' figurine made under a licence from James Robertson & Sons and retailing on release at £180. The 'Golly' figurine went on to make £250+ on eBay and still commands this price today. Given that it's a limited edition of 2000 this is quite amazing and largely due to the fact that it is a classic character, made under licence by Royal Doulton when it was producing in Great Britain. These are all the key elements to a successful collectable – it also helped of course that this was the first in a range that is still being broadened out today.

Conclusion

- No limited edition is guaranteed to increase in value. Most items that are collectable gain this status once they are no longer generally available – so always buy what you like rather than gambling on what may or may not make a fortune.
- As a general rule the smaller the edition size, the quicker it will sell out, the faster it will become collectable, the more people will want it, the quicker the demand will outstrip supply, and the more chance there is that the price will rise rapidly compared to the original purchase price.
- Always avoid so-called 'limited editions' that run into thousands or are not clearly recognisable as having a limited production.
- Keep your eye out for anything that is quickly withdrawn

after being released and remember to invest time in watching how the market moves and what items sell very well. Then ask yourself why these items are more sought-after than others.

- Whenever you purchase a collectable remember to keep the receipt, the box, the limited-edition certificate, and any other documentation relating to the piece.

CHAPTER THREE

SELLING AT BOOT SALES

Having separated the stuff to bin from the boot sale booty, it's time to prepare for the event itself. Anyone can do a car boot sale; it's no great mystery and there's no right or wrong way to do things but there are certainly some steps that can be taken to help make the maximum money on the day. As a journalist first and foremost, my golden rule is to always do my research and this really should apply to just about everything in life if you are going to have the advantage over others.

Finding the Right Boot Sale

As there are hundreds of boot sales across the country it's vital that you choose the right one for the items that you are selling. Many boot sales today are arguably also markets.

Officially, to be a market a proper licence is required but many boot sales allow market traders on their sites providing they are not selling counterfeit goods, anything else illegal, or anything that requires a licence. The only way to learn which boot sales are best is to visit them in person ahead of actually selling.

Local newspapers list the boot sales taking place near you in their 'What's On' sections and there are also specialist publications, such as *The Car Boot Calendar*, that list every single venue across the country with opening times, details of the sort of boot sale it is, and contact numbers. In general, though, nothing can replace the experience of actually visiting a site to see what's on offer and whether or not it's suitable for the items that you have. Word of mouth is a great help too. Ask workmates, mums and dads at the school gates and friends who go to boot sales which ones they think are good and why. Remember, if a friend has dedicated his life to finding a Harry Potter first edition for £3 and then selling it for £15,000 (which happened three years ago), he will be looking for boot sales where there are plenty of people selling children's books dating from 1997 (when *Harry Potter and the Philosopher's Stone* was first published). A school mum may well recommend a boot sale where she was able to shift all the children's old clothes and toys and return with £200 in her pocket. Nevertheless, whatever their motivation, they will certainly have a view on whether a boot sale is stacked up with sellers or a bargaining ground for buyers.

There are still many bargains to be had when hunting around boot sales.

When you visit your first boot sale you should:

Be prepared to cancel any arrangements for the night before; set the alarm for at least forty-five minutes before the opening time of the boot sale to allow for queues getting into the venue; and have a very early night. Wear plenty of layers whatever the weather or forecast. Arriving at a venue at 5 a.m. will be cold, whether it's summer or winter, but in the summer I've filmed in 100 degrees by midday so you don't want to be stuck in a winter jumper unable to strip down without embarrassment.

Check out the local area. Does it appear to be fairly afflu-ent? If so, the chances are that the sort of items being sold will be pretty good and that the money people are prepared to spend at the venue will be more than most. For example, Ascot car boot sale in Berkshire is well known for having plenty of 'ladies who lunch' boot-sellers clearing out their designer wardrobes at amazingly good prices. Similarly, lots of antique dealers also attend with vans and lorries full of pretty good antique furniture because they know lots of the local buyers from the Ascot area are not short of a bob or two to spend.

Take note of the entrances. There are always separate entrances for buyers and sellers. Usually sellers are given the priority as they have to park up and set up their stalls. Is there a queue of sellers waiting to get a pitch? If so, that's good news as it means there is demand from sellers to attend this boot sale which implies they have had success there in the past. Similarly, if there is a queue of people waiting to get in to buy that is also a sign that these people have had good buys here before and have come out with money to spend providing they find bargain buys.

Note the charges made by the boot sale organiser for buyers' entry and pitches for sellers. It's not necessarily the cheapest charges that make for the most profitable boot sale. Some organisers who are launching new boot sales will keep charges low to encourage people to attend. Increasingly, with boot sales being held almost on top of each other – there are five within an eight-mile radius of where I live – boot sale organisers are having to be competitive with their charges. More established boot sales can afford, if they are good venues, to keep their rates up because they know that people will always return. Some boot sales make no charge for going into the venue, others charge up to £1 per person with reductions for OAPs and children while pitches can range from £6 for local school boot sale venues to £20 for large lorries or vans attending well-established boot sales. Those who really get into boot sale selling and plan to attend the same boot sale on a weekly basis should chat to the organisers who will sometimes reserve pitch locations and offer a discount to those who pay in advance for a few weeks or months.

<u>**Chat to buyers and sellers**</u> to find out what they think about this particular boot sale, good and bad. Everyone needs a coffee or tea boost to rest their weary feet at a boot sale and there's nothing like queuing at the burger van with others to hear plenty of boot sale tales and stories of great finds, hits and misses. Stop at any stalls with similar items to those you plan to sell and ask the seller what made them choose this particular venue. Have they stalled out here before? Was it successful? Would they come back again? What sort of money are people spending? There can be a great difference across the country when it comes to the amount of money people spend at boot sales. In Melton Mowbray, for example, we filmed an episode of *Car Booty* at a covered-market boot sale. The boot sale was a great venue for buyers because the general norm was that people rarely seemed to pay more than a few pounds for even the most choice items – but that's not good news for the sellers. Our contributors found it a struggle to sell a great framed print for £1 although they did shift a 1940s Mickey Mouse wristwatch for £140 – clearly there's money there but getting it out of people's pockets can be a lot easier in some counties than others. At the Wansted Rugby Club boot sale near Chigwell (the village made famous by Dorian in the television series *Birds of a Feather*) sellers can command £90 for a Burberry second-hand but genuine handbag, and £30 for Burberry jumpers and other designer gear,

which, I am pretty sure, would sit there all day at Melton Mowbray.

Assess the weather implications. Some boot sales, such as Clitheroe, have the option of both outside pitches and inside pitches. Don't get too excited, it's not glamorous. The site is a cattle market which means that there is hard-standing, i.e. a car park that readily converts into boot sale pitches outside and cattle stalls on concrete under a tin roof inside. Clearly, if rain is forecast the vast majority of boot-sellers will want indoor pitches. Many regulars will get priority, so you may have to allow even more time and be prepared to queue for up to an hour just to get a pitch. Even then, be prepared for disappointment and a wet day outside if all the pitches are gone inside by the time it's your turn to get in. Most boot sales don't even have this option. In Essex, the ground is notorious for being clay soil, which often gets waterlogged. While it has to be pretty bad for the Stevenson's Farm boot sale to cancel, the Dunton car boot sale at Brentwood is often called off the night before if there has been a downpour, as the pitch simply becomes too waterlogged to cope with the onslaught of cars. As a result, Stevenson's Farm can be even more packed out with the boot-sellers who turn up at Dunton only to find that it has been cancelled. You can check with the organiser about their weather policy and you need to have a telephone number you can call which will provide a message the night before outlining whether or not the boot sale is to take place. It's clearly worth having a back-up venue given that the time spent sorting out stuff for the boot sale and packing the car the night before will be wasted if the boot sale you choose is not on.

Consider the time of year. The first boot sales usually get under way at the end of February and believe me they can be a bitter experience. We filmed *Car Booty* at the Milton Keynes Bowl venue in minus 3 degrees and snow! Not to be recommended, although both our families sold their stuff and there were plenty of buyers there spending money. They were wrapped up in skiwear – I alone was in a pair of high-heeled boots with a pretty cream coat! Many boot sales which were established before 1997 have the right to hold as many boot sales as they like during the year, providing the sites are maintained, required first aid is available and police liaison is conducted to ensure that the venue does not create a traffic hazard. However, those established after this time are subject to planning laws. This means they must apply to the local council for planning permission to hold a boot sale event. The local council will grant permission for only a certain number of boot sales to be held during the year. The clock starts ticking from the first boot sale to take place in the calendar year. Therefore, if permission is given for twenty boot sales to be held, and the organiser starts with the first boot sale in March the planning permission will run out by July, i.e. four Sundays a month in March, April, May, June, July equals twenty boot sales. Given such restrictions and the fact that, in general, our best weather is in August and September, many organisers delay holding their first boot sale until the Easter weekend at the earliest. In this way they have a good chance of holding the maximum number of boot sales without having to cancel for bad weather. You will need to find out when the boot sales start and ask the organisers whether some weekends are better than others to stall out.

Peter Stevenson, who runs Stevenson's Farm, explains:

We find that our busiest boot sale is always the Sunday before the kids go back to school. It's packed out with sellers, particularly, of course, mums clearing out the kiddies' wardrobes before the school year. Having said that, the Bank Holiday weekends are always packed too with buyers and sellers at Easter and in August. Many people pop down to the boot sale before Sunday lunch and where we are located, being so near to Southend, means they can go onto the seafront later in the day as part of the Bank Holiday celebrations. We've even had coach parties of pensioners turn up who are on their way for a day out at Southend and have forced the coach driver to stop because they want to trawl the boot sale first!

Having decided on the boot sale you think will be the best one at which to sell the items you have, it's time to prepare for the big boot sale day. For those of you who really cannot stomach the early start, bear in mind that some boot sales do take place in the afternoon. There's one in Essex that many early-bird boot sale buyers go to last thing on a Sunday. It is called, appropriately enough, Lazybones and starts at 1 p.m. On one trip there I managed to buy a stunning box full of Brittain's zoo animal figures from the 1950s for just £4, which was not bad considering there were more than forty different types of animal in the box. But generally it would be safe to assume that by the afternoon a lot of boot sale buyers have had enough, and dealers may well have run out of money to spend, so be a lazybones at your peril.

Things to Remember

Here's a basic checklist of what you need in order to be well prepared for your first boot sale:

A sense of humour. This is a fun day out for all the family to enjoy. It is an adventure that should include a treasure trove of cash and coins by the end of the day, so make sure you have this attitude as it will carry you through the day as people try to haggle with you over the odd five-pence piece!

Wrap it and pack it (the night before). Never leave the wrapping and packing until the morning of the boot sale. It's far too early and it takes far longer than anyone ever estimates. Just think about moving house and you have the same problems on a miniature scale. Everyone underestimates the size of removal van they need, so with boot sales people overestimate just how much boot sale booty they can get in a Mini Cooper. No one ever realises how much stuff they have until they have to pack it up to move nor how long the packing process will take and it's exactly the same for boot sales. Allow plenty of time the day before to sort out your items in an orderly fashion. The last thing packed should be the pasting table. I would suggest:

- Glass is wrapped in old newspaper and boxed for protection – any old cardboard box will do and most supermarkets or shops are only too happy for you to have their old delivery boxes. Be warned though, many have contracts with waste-paper companies and the days when supermarkets were piled high with boxes out the back are long gone so you will need to ask at the beginning of the week for boxes to be put by for you in order to have plenty available by the weekend. Always check that the box has a firm base and is not likely to collapse once filled. Mark the box up with what's inside so that you know what each box contains when you get to the boot sale. This way, if a buyer asks 'Have you any glass?' you can immediately locate the box and the glass you have for the buyer's perusal.

Top tip: If the boot sale is hard-standing, i.e. on concrete, the cardboard boxes once unpacked should be broken up and the cardboard laid around your stall. This is an old dealer's trick, as cardboard underfoot acts as an absorption blanket for cold and damp, thus helping to prevent your feet aching halfway through the day from all the standing around.

- China should be packed carefully with plates and saucers kept together with a layer of paper between each one. Bear in mind that the print comes off on your hands and rubs off onto nearby items so ensure that you don't pack all the china and then white linen without washing your hands. Always wash china and glass either by hand if it is not dishwasher proof or through the dishwasher in order for it to be bright and gleaming. Dust may hint at age, but it also is a flag for hagglers to try and knock the price down.

Top tip: Consider pricing up your items with little adhesive price tickets, but make sure these are tickets that can be easily removed without causing damage to the item itself. Try a code system rather than an actual price, e.g. A=1, B=2, C=3, etc. This way an item you price at £12 would be marked 'AB' allowing you to remember what price you want. By not actually revealing the price in pounds you are not risking putting people off because they immediately see the price and think it is too dear.

- Small items including jewellery, watches, coins and badges for example, should be attached to cushions for display purposes but also so that you can locate them and keep an eye on them. Other options, if you have the time, include getting an old picture frame with glass and laying this over a tray. The depth of the tray means the items can be displayed but the glass frame will prevent people 'lifting' items and means they have to ask to see a piece so you can ensure that none of your goods 'walk'.

Top tip: If you are thinking of becoming a regular boot-seller, then make sure you talk to all your customers and find out why they are interested in or buying the items you are selling. This way you can get an idea of what regular boot-sale buyers attending this boot sale are looking for and make sure that you have the right items for the right buyers next time.

- Toys are best sold complete with the original box. Obviously nowadays, and depending on the size of your home, it's virtually impossible to keep the boxes for large toys but the difference in price can be huge. An unboxed but complete Thunderbirds Tracy Island toy may make £5–£10 but a boxed version can fetch £20. Toys that are from the 1960s and in good condition with their original boxes, particularly Barbie, Ken, Sindy and Action Man, should be priced accordingly and possibly sold at auction or on eBay rather than at a boot sale. And don't feel inclined to seal boxes with Sellotape – this is a nightmare for collectors as it often damages the box itself and they will expect a discount for any tape damage.

Top tip: If you are also bitten by the boot sale buying bug look out for stalls manned by men or women who are clearly over thirty. This generation is the one most likely to be selling off old toys that could well be collectable or of value. At my very first *Boot Sale Challenge* filming day I spotted a woman of about my age who was selling her old toys and quickly acquired a 1960s Merrythought Golly and 1960s Noddy doll complete with hat with bell for £1 the pair. This was back in 1997, when one of the experts on the programme, Mr H – Paul Hetchin – immediately offered £12 for the Noddy and £12 for the Golly, an easy profit but one I had to decline. I still have both toys today.

Clothes are best washed, ironed, protected in cellophane and hung on a hanging rail at the boot sale. Clearly, not everyone will have a hanging rail, but the better clothes are displayed the better price you will get. I have bought designer coats for my four-year-old at boot sales for £2 simply because they were tossed onto a groundsheet among lots of old clothes. I have also paid £15 for a Moschino two-piece designer suit that had been freshly dry cleaned (that's £12 worth of dry cleaning) and hung on a hanging rail. Ask around friends to see whether you can borrow one for the day and check with the boot sale organiser as some, such as Peter Stevenson, will provide industrial clothes rails for hire at a small charge.

Top tip: Don't ask too much for children's clothes. There is no VAT (charged at 17.5% of the retail price) payable on new children's clothes, which is why they are always comparatively cheaper to buy than adult clothes and you risk making your second-hand kids' clothes too expensive. Remember also that supermarkets now have their own children's ranges and with the price war going on between
the big stores some, Tesco for example, are selling brand-new children's polo shirts for just £2. So don't try and charge £2 for a comparable second-hand version.

<u>Don't sell electrical items</u> unless you have either had them checked by an electrician, which is expensive, or have cut the lead and plug off the item. The law is such that should someone buy an electrical item from you and then go home, plug it in and blow their fuses or, worse still, electrocute themselves, you are responsible. If in doubt you should check with your council's local trading standards office to see whether an item is suitable for selling. Similarly, *Which?* magazine recommends that people do not sell children's car seats as there is no guarantee when buying such items second-hand that they are fit for the job.

Top tip: If you have any doubts about the items you plan to sell, don't risk it. Trading standards officers and the police often visit boot sales and I have been at boot sales raided by trading standards where counterfeit videos and goods were being sold. Private individuals selling the odd home video copy of a film taped from television are unlikely to be 'raided' – but those who are clearly bulk-selling items that are obviously fake or counterfeit are breaking the law and face prosecution. It's not worth it. Similarly, most boot sale organisers reserve the right to refuse entry to or remove those selling such goods or brand-new items bought in bulk from wholesalers.

<u>Apply common sense to the items you are selling</u>. It's never a good idea to sell knives, stunt guns or other items that are clearly either dangerous or potentially controversial. I know several people who make a point of collecting vintage fur jackets and stoles from boot sales but on the other hand I have also overhead people making very pointed comments about such sales given the sensitivity about wearing fur.

Top tip: It's a brave person who does a boot sale on their own. Apart from the call of nature (which can mean you have to abandon your stall and take the risk that people might help themselves without paying), it's more fun with a friend, partner or family. It means that you can take breaks and have a walk around in the summer sunshine or take it in turns to take cover in the car in the pouring rain. It also means that if you do encounter less than friendly buyers or hagglers who hassle then you have back-up.

Never underestimate what will sell. I have seen other peoples' sets of false teeth for sale and sold at a boot sale! Never underestimate what won't sell either. Some of my best bargains have been items abandoned at the end of the boot sale, including a wonderful Victorian fireplace, which was left in the middle of a Kent boot sale in the summer after we were filming *Car Booty*. Never one to let pride get in the way I put it in the boot and two days later the photographer from *TV Quick* magazine spotted it in the garden and now has it installed in the living room of his East London townhouse. I cannot bear to see anything go to waste and was delighted that it had a new home. The photographer offered £150 for it because he had been looking for such an example and had not been able to locate one with such a simple design, despite having a budget of up to £500!

Top tip: At the end of a boot sale there are always people prepared to go through the bins and skips for items abandoned by those who simply don't want to take their old 'junk' home. These people are rather disparagingly referred to as 'scratchers' but frankly that doesn't stop me. It can be, providing you get permission from the boot sale organiser, a very rewarding experience. I have found some wonderful children's books in excellent condition simply dumped in bins around boot sales. Most organisers are responsible for ensuring that the field, which is often rented from a farmer, is left as it was found and so have to clear away all rubbish. This means simply scooping it up and dumping it in skips to be taken away to refuse dumps. Peter Stevenson, boot sale organiser, adds: 'I own my site, so I have a large number of skips on the site into which the bins are emptied after every boot sale. I've found some wonderful items, including a fabulous Troika vase which had been dumped in a bin and I saw sticking out of the skip. Remarkably, it was undamaged and valued at £120.

This vase was found in a skip at the end of a boot sale in Basildon, Essex. It is worth £120.

Don't forget to pack a pasting table. These can be purchased from most DIY stores for around £10 or hired on site at the boot sale (check first). Take two if you think that you have so much stuff it will never get onto one table or might cause the table will collapse under the weight. Consider packing a deckchair or patio chair too, as it's a long day to just stand up.

Top tip: Given the early start, by 8 a.m. it feels as if it's time for a Sunday lunch. Most vegetarians, health nuts or those who simply cannot face boot sale burgers, are unlikely to find much to buy at a boot sale that will meet their requirements. Consider taking a packed lunch and a flask of tea or coffee and plenty of water. Boot sale organisers often charge a considerable premium to the boot sale burger-van proprietors because they make a lot of money during the day supplying fast food (burgers can cost anything from £1–£2.50), cans of fizzy drink (50p–£1 and even more for proper branded drinks) and teas and coffees (50p–£1 a time). It's worth the effort of taking your own supplies on the basis that most people want to make as much money as possible and it's very easy to get through £10 before you know it in drinks and food at a boot sale.

<u>Have plenty of change</u>. You'll be surprised how much you'll need and how many people want to hand over £5, £10 and £20 notes first thing in the morning for items costing 50p–£1. If you have a piggy bank at home, raid it for coins of all denominations plus several £5 notes and a couple of £10 notes so that you don't lose a sale simply because you have no change. Alternatively, go to any high-street bank with your 'float' money and ask them to break it down into bags of coins with several £5 notes. There should be no charge for this service and the banks will provide you with plastic bags for the currency which makes life easier at the sale. Make sure you have a secure box or money belt to hold both your float and the money you take in.

Top tip: Beware of buyers with £50 notes who spend around £20. Many years ago I did a boot sale at Willow Tree Farm in Rainham in Essex and sold, to a very nice old couple, a pair of Sylvac vases and several Wade items for a total of £22. They paid with a £50 note and I gave them £28 change. Later that day, I visited my local 24-hour supermarket and was horrified when the cashier held the £50 note under a special detector machine and revealed it to be a fake. My father worked in print all his life and even he found it difficult to spot this superb forgery for what it was. Legally, once you are aware a note is fake, you must hand it in to the police station. It is then sent to the Bank of England where it is destroyed if fake and returned if genuine. It is an offence knowingly to attempt to pass off or spend any fake money and, unfortunately, it is often very hard to detect. The Bank of England has its own free leaflet on how to check notes for the correct markings but it's often too late for boot sale sellers – the only rule that really works is to beware of people who may seem rather too keen to pay for a few low-cost items with a £50 note.

<u>Pick your boot sale pitch.</u> Once you have arrived at the boot sale you will be directed by the organiser's employees to a pitch. Unless you have made special arrangements with the organiser, this will simply be the next in line on a row as the pressure is on for the organisers to get everyone in and stalled out. Remember you are not the only seller, the people either side of you are selling too, so don't be too greedy with your pitch and spill over with boxes and items into their area. Be considerate and remember that not everyone wants to hear your car stereo pumping out classical opera, Cliff Richard or rap renditions at full blast at 5 a.m. in the morning – or at any point in the day for that matter. Make the most of the opportunity to meet new people and share the experiences you have with your new boot-selling neighbours – the great thing about boot sales is that they are so much more than money-making

means of clearing junk. They are entire communities with a camaraderie of their own which can help forge friendships, romances and if nothing else make the day a right good laugh.

Top tip: Many boot sale organisers have learnt from their past mistakes – when dealers were allowed in and would follow cars as they pitched up, crawl into the car boots pulling out items and generally hassling sellers into parting with pieces before they were fully prepared for the day's selling. Now many have a policy where dealers are not allowed into car boots and must keep a respectable distance until the seller is ready to start selling. Alternatively, or if in doubt about the organiser's policy, simply park up, lock up and go and get a coffee before you set up your stall. Within half an hour the dealers will have moved on to the next new row and you can return to your pitch and set up at a leisurely pace. The dealers may well be looking for a killing first thing by pouncing into car boots, but most then take a second walk around so you are unlikely to lose any sales by delaying the start of proceedings. You will, however, save yourself a lot of hassle. On the very first boot sale I did, people were quite literally following my car and climbing into the car boot trying to buy the foot pump and the groundsheet, which weren't even for sale.

<u>Be prepared to haggle</u>. Remember the reason you are doing a boot sale is to clear stuff that you no longer want. Therefore, within reason any money you get for these items is a bonus, so don't cut off your nose to spite your face if someone makes a reasonable offer. On the other hand, if you have

genuinely valuable items, or goods which you would be happy to take home unless you get the right price, stick to your asking price but don't be offended if people offer you far less than you'd hoped for. That's the nature of boot sales. I was at a boot sale at Nuthill Fruit Farm in Guildford in Surrey filming *Car Booty* when a lady buyer asked the price for three handbags. All were nearly new and they consisted of two gorgeous brown Kelly-style ostrich leather bags which had to be worth £80–£100 each and a black Radley bag (retail price £120). The seller was asking £7 for the three, which was clearly, to a girl such as myself with a handbag fetish, the bargain of the year. However, the potential lady buyer would offer only £5

These three handbags were a bargain at just £7 and I paid the full asking price without any hesitation as they are worth at least £280 for the lot.

for the three and refused to budge. So did the seller. The result was a sale of three handbags for the asking price of £7 – to me.

Top tip: Lots of children get hours of enjoyment from boot sales. They learn the value of money and are able to buy toys for pocket-money prices and start collections of their own as a result. It's a great thing, which I'd like to see encouraged more in order to help children learn a sense of responsibility together with an appreciation of money and what it will or won't buy. Clearly, children who are trying to buy items for themselves should be encouraged to haggle and few boot sale sellers can resist the pleas of a youngster desperate to secure a soft toy for their last ten-pence piece. However, some harder collectors and dealers are not averse to sending their children to stalls to haggle for more expensive collectable items. It may sound cynical, but I've seen enough boot sale buyers in my time to know that this happens and is a practised tactic among some dealers and obsessive, yet scrooge-like, collectors.

Finally, enjoy the day, don't count your money up until you get home as this not only alerts others to the money you have made but also spoils the surprise at the end of the day when you tot up all the change and realise you've made a mint! Oh, and do make sure you have cancelled all Sunday evening invitations as you will be totally exhausted!

Conclusion

- Always sell at a boot sale that has been recommended to you or one that you have visited previously to make sure you are happy that the venue is suitable for the items you have on offer.
- Take plenty of change, comfortable shoes and lots of layers of clothing to keep warm/cool. You should also take a chair to sit on, and don't forget the pasting table. When you arrive at the boot sale, get a coffee first before setting out your stall so you don't get harassed by the first wave of dealers.
- Remember that you can always lower your price throughout the day. But you should start off by asking the top price,

and be prepared to meet people who make sensible offers halfway.

- If possible, get a friend or family member to help you as it can be a tough day doing a boot sale on your own, as well as quite problematic if you need to pop to the loo or get something to eat!
- Take plenty of plastic bags and newspaper to wrap up the items you are selling for your buyers – and remember service with a smile goes a long way.

CHAPTER FOUR

BUYING AT BOOT SALES

The thrill of buying at boot sales revolves around the whole idea that somewhere out there is a fortune waiting to be found, the bargain of a lifetime that will make the buyer richer in a few moments than they could possibly be by working for a year or two. The fact that for many years now there really have been some fantastic boot sale finds, which have made a fortune at auction, simply helps fuel people's desire to get up ridiculously early in the morning and trawl as many boot sales as possible in the hope and belief that one day, at one boot sale they will find the Holy Grail, the elusive item that they alone recognise has a rarity and value far beyond their wildest dreams. Just last year, Christie's film and entertainment auction at South Kensington in London saw a rare Imperial stormtrooper's helmet sell for £13,145. This was one of only six made for George Lucas, the director of the *Star Wars* movies, as a visual aid to support his final pitch to film company executives to obtain funding for the very first 1977 *Star Wars* film. The helmet was then kept and used in the film and also in the 1980 sequel *The Empire Strikes Back*. The price realised at auction was even more phenomenal given that the vendor had purchased this piece twelve years before from a London boot sale for £40.

At Bonhams five years ago a Limehouse porcelain sauceboat dating from 1746–48 sold for £9,200. This previously unrecorded piece was bought at a car boot sale for just 50p, while a nocturnal found in a bag of old wooden bits and pieces bought from a Surrey boot sale for £15 made £4,300. The instrument, which dates from 1730 and was used by sailors to take observations from the stars to tell the time at night, looked like a wooden ruler to the untrained eye but proved that some-one somewhere had taken the time to specialise and learn a lot in order to realise its potential.

At a boot sale in Essex, Martin Donovan was waiting as a lady unloaded her car. Standing at one end of the table, he decided to go to the other end to look at something. As he did this he saw her pull out a bowl and place it where he had originally been standing. A dealer snapped it up instantly, and paid the 50p asking price. Martin was in the wrong place at the wrong time as the bowl was by Moorcroft in the 'Anemone' pattern and was worth £300.

Then there are the heart-moving rather than economically pro-ductive boot sale finds, such as that of the schoolgirl who found her favourite cuddly toy at a boot sale six years after dropping it at a bus stop. Stephanie Richardson, nine, and mum Carol, thirty-five, both boot sale enthusiasts, spotted the furry dog at a car boot sale in 2003 for 25p. Inside the toy was a pen mark that Stephanie had made many years earlier. She had never given up hope of finding the toy she called 'Daisy' which had been lost in Rhyl, North Wales back in 1997.

So how do you spot a piece of Limehouse porcelain or a nocturnal or a Delft cup? What should you be prepared to pay and where is the best place to resell such unbelievable bargains and cash in on your good fortune? The simple answer is that if it was quite as easy as it sounds even more people would be out every Sunday at boot sales. The bargain boot sale buy appears deceptively simple but hides years of reading up on all sorts of subjects, keeping abreast with news, markets, the economy and the areas of collectability which can often go through booms and busts, and a lot of time spent in windy, rainy, cold locations fighting off other dealers and the bitter cold in an effort to locate a bargain buy. In other words, nothing is that easy: it all involves a lot of work and time but it can also be great fun and the chances are you will meet some wonderfully colourful characters and find lots of interesting, if not hugely profitable, items along the way.

At every boot sale I have ever been to or filmed at there have been easily identifiable dealers, or enthusiast collectors busily flying through the field in the search of their elusive booty. They are looking for items that they know are rare or valuable and that they are hoping to find in among the cleared clutter of people's lives. Record dealers and collectors, for example, are easy to spot. They are always rifling through record boxes at a furious rate, pulling out certain albums and disregarding others at a rate of knots. They are oblivious to everyone else around them, anything else on the stall and have a tunnel vision that is really quite remarkable to witness. They don't even talk to each other as they go around the car boot sale but you often see one or two finally walking upright, rather than bent double over a box on the ground, with a satisfied smile and hugging a piece of vinyl that I have to admit I would easily have passed by with no regard to its rarity or value. However, even I know that the Beatles *Sergeant Pepper's Lonely Hearts Club Band* LP signed by all four Beatles sold at Christie's in New York three years ago for the equivalent of £38,000.

Then there are the generalists who are clearly having a ball at the boot sale, snapping up all sorts of items that they think are bargains without much regard to budget or boot space. They are completely laden down with bags by 8 a.m. and on their umpteenth trip back to the car ready to refill their trolley, rucksack and laundry bags with more booty. These are the amateur booters-cum-dealers who are just starting to realise that their money goes a long way bargaining at boot sales and they have heard plenty of tales about people who are making thousands a month by reselling on eBay. Most of these people have yet to actually make the step from boot sale buyer to eBay entrepreneur, but they have no doubt that their fortune will be found by following this path. Those who have come through this stage and are now actively selling on eBay are likely to be keeping the details of what they are looking for very close to their chest.

So how do you get the best boot sale bargains?

Locations and Times

Be prepared to visit plenty of boot sales on a continuous basis to increase your chances of finding a real bargain buy. Even the same boot sale at the same location can vary greatly from week to week and it's always worth venturing further afield. Items that are hard to find down South may be easier to locate at boot sales in the North and vice versa. I've found that prices can vary greatly at boot sales further North. At Clitheroe Cattle Market boot sale I bought a Spitting Image board game for 50p which I had seen at another boot sale in Epsom priced at £10. Dating from the 1980s and featuring Ronald Reagan, Mikhail Gorbachov and Margaret Thatcher in typical satirical Spitting Image mode, this game is a must for both Spitting Image collectors and those who collect political memorabilia and it can realise £20 on eBay.

Certain board games have a value provided they are classics like Spitting Image.

Some boot-salers argue that the smaller boot sales, such as those held at local village halls and schools, are the most fertile ground for bargains simply because people are turning out for a good cause; others suggest that it's better to go to the larger boot sales because there is a wider selection and therefore a better chance of getting a sought-after item.

Personally, having been to so many boot sales, I always enjoy any that are slightly different. Many years ago, I went to a stately home boot sale at Glemham Hall in Suffolk. The queues to get in were horrendous and Bonhams was on site to prevent anyone selling hidden treasure at a bargain price, but it was great fun and an amazing experience, even though the prices being asked were similar to those you expect at an antiques fair. Amazingly, one of the best resources for stately home boot sales is *Country Life* magazine, which is a weekly up-market glossy publication. The June issue of this magazine often covers the various car boot sales taking place at locations ranging from Cholmondeley Castle in Cheshire to Glemham Hall and this information can also be found at www.countrylife.co.uk. Christie's consultant John Hardy, who attended the boot sale at Cholmondeley Castle, was quoted in *Country Life* as saying he had purchased a fine silk top hat for £15 and a Flight Barr and Barr Worcester Vase for £8. My favourite is the Henley-on-Thames annual RNLI boot sale, which started in 1981 and is now in its twenty-fourth year. It is always held on the second Sunday in September; it raised £270 in its first year but by last year had added £9,500 to the RNLI coffers. There are about 400 car-boot-sellers and the event takes place on the field better known for hosting the Henley Royal Regatta – indeed it is the Henley Royal Regatta Committee that kindly agree to this special boot sale taking place. It's well worth the visit not just because the location is so stunning but also because the range of stalls and objects is so vast.

Top tip: If you get to a boot sale after the early rush, don't worry, it's not always a case of the early bird catches the worm, as Su Cowen a regular boot-saler explains, 'My all-time best boot sale buy was a stylised 1950s wall plaque of a beautiful lady, which I purchased for £3 at Barleylands Boot Fair in Essex and sold to a lady in Austria through eBay for £250. I snapped up the item because I really liked it but it's worth pointing out that this was also at 11 a.m. in the morning, some four hours after the boot sale had opened!'

Preparing for a Boot Sale Buying Trip

It's vital to be comfortable at a boot sale as you're going to be walking for miles in what could be a wide range of temperatures. Whether it's winter or summer, it's important to wear layers of clothing either for warmth or so you can gradually remove them as the sun and the temperature rises during the day. Go for:

Really comfortable shoes or wellies in the winter, as most boot sale fields are pretty muddy and can get really sodden even in the late spring. It's also worth investing in a pedometer just to see how far you actually end up walking – you'll be amazed and delighted as it's a great form of exercise.

Wearing a hat will help contain body heat and then reduce it as it gets warmer and it is particularly useful for the inevitable showers. A Dri-as-a-bone or Barbour stetson-style hat is not a fashion accessory, it is a vital piece of equipment that allows the rain to run off without drenching you and does away with cumbersome umbrellas, leaving your hands free to rummage.

Sun cream is vital in the summer as it's really easy to get sunburn and sunstroke without even realising it as you are walking around.

Sunglasses and hayfever tablets are a must if you suffer from allergies. In the summer, boot sale fields can get really dusty as the cars move round, and the fields themselves are often near crops of rapeseed oil which is a known source of allergens for some people.

Other useful hints for buyers are:

Consider taking your own sandwiches and bottled water or a flask – you'll save money this way for those bargain buys.

Make sure you have plenty of change before you go as it will be too early in the morning to change up banknotes. Boot sale organisers, sellers and burger-bar vendors will not welcome large banknotes offered up for items costing pence.

Take your cash card just in case there is a bargain there that is going to cost more money than you have taken with you. Most organisers will know where the nearest cash machine is located and if it's a real bargain buy, the seller will usually allow you to leave a deposit for a set time period while you go to get the rest of the money.

Empty your car out the night before and put the back seats down. This way, you're not going to return to your car clutching bags of bargains only to find that you've got the garden rubbish in the boot ready to go down the dump and no room for anything else.

Always keep some strong carrier bags and bubble wrap in the glove compartment as not every seller will have come armed with hoards of carrier bags for your car booty. The bubble wrap is useful for delicate items or for small items that may get lost at the bottom of a bag.

Invest in an eyeglass; they can easily be purchased for under £10. Go for a x10 magnification. This will help you spot silver marks on items and general damage, such as hairline cracks on china and chips on glass items. Generally speaking, sellers don't object to potential buyers giving items the once over through an eyeglass and it can prevent you parting with cash for items you think are perfect only to discover they are damaged when you get home.

In the winter, take a torch with you, as many of the boot sales open in the dark and this can help you not only see your way round but also scan stalls for potential bargains. If you shine a beam from a torch into a ceramic item it should also show up any cracks or splits that might not be easy to spot at such an early hour. There are slim, easy to carry, pro-beam torches complete with their own batteries available from Marks and Spencer at £2.50 each or from most trekking and camping shops.

Again, in the winter, it is also worth investing in the hand-warmer packs that are heat-generating. Simply shaking the sachet causes the heat to come from the bag and this will help keep you warm on the coldest of days. Again these can be purchased at around 75p–£1.50 a time from camping shops but avoid the ones that need to be pre-heated in a microwave as you're unlikely to be this organised at 4 a.m.

Plan your route if you are going to be visiting several boot sales and check the weather and road reports the night before on teletext. This will help you avoid any nasty road works or traffic jams coming back from boot sales or on your way to other boot sales.

Take a notebook or dictaphone so you can keep an ongoing record of how much you have spent and on what. Don't expect receipts at boot sales and this will be the only way you will be able to record how much you paid – vital when working out how much money you have made when you sell the pieces on again.

Just before you get to the boot sale it's worth stopping at a petrol station and filling up the car. This gives you the chance to use the loo as the facilities at most boot sales leave much to be desired. The Saturday boot sale held at Denham on the M40/M25 junction can have up to 600 stalls and 5,000 people in attendance – all sharing two mobile toilets.

Top tip: Always take a rucksack with you as this enables you to stash your bargains on your back, leaving your hands free to rummage around and check out further buys. Most stallholders will happily look after larger items for you until you are ready to go and pick them up, providing you pay for them. However, do check what time the stallholder plans to leave the boot sale as you cannot expect them to wait for you, and make a mental note of where the stall is in the boot sale or you may never find it again.

Identify and Try Different Niche Markets

You have to kiss a lot of frogs in life to find a prince, and with making money from boot sales and on the Internet the same rule applies. You cannot go wrong by going to plenty of boot sales, seeing what people are selling, what people are buying and taking a chance on a few different items from children's toys to china, books to baby clothes. List them on eBay, and find what sells best for the most money. Over time, you will make contact with regular boot sale buyers and eBay buyers who will give you plenty of feedback and information about the sort of things they are looking for. Immediately, you can start drawing up an informal database of people you know are on the lookout for specific items. This way, you too can put the word out and start looking for these items. If you find anything suitable you will know that you can sell it on, to one of your regular customers, for a quick profit. The quicker the turn-around between buying an item and selling it, the better your cash flow and the more money you will have to reinvest. The worst scenario is to have spent your money on items that are either not selling or not selling for a profit. Holding out for a set profit can be the worst thing to do – just remember, every-one sells items at some point for a loss just to get a percentage of their money back.

Only through trial and error will you find an area that suits your own tastes and has a market where there is money to be made. Most people currently buying from boot sales and selling on the Internet are specialists in certain areas and have moved on from the very first area they specialised in.

Top tip: Jo from South Woodford is an absolute boot sale fanatic and says that boot sales in West London and Essex are excellent for buying, particularly if you check out under the tables and are prepared to rummage around the boxes that appear to hold nothing but 'junk'. By rooting around boxes under tables she's found an authentic Prada bag for 50p and a Venetian mirror for £1.50, which she sold immediately to another dealer for £12. She says, 'My favourite boot sale is the one held each month at Chiswick where you get some amazing stuff and many celebrities including Rula Lenska have been known to stall out.'

Identifying Stalls

TOYS

Collectors have found original Barbie and Sindy furniture still in their boxes for under £1, Gollies for 50p and even a talking Noddy from the 1960s for 50p, since valued for £60. The toys from this generation are now highly sought after by collectors who are busy buying back their childhood toys that went to a boot sale many years ago!

Regular boot sale buyer Su Cowen explains:

Last year, I went to a boot sale in Essex and bought a collection of vintage Sindy dolls and found in the box a Patch doll too. Amazingly, within a week at another boot sale I had found an original Patch outfit for 10p so I dressed the Patch doll in the original Patch clothes and it sold on eBay for

Patch was introduced as Sindy's sister and was bought at a boot sale for £1, later to sell on eBay for £100.

£100. One of the Sindy dolls turned out to be an early strawberry blonde Sindy and made £65. On another occasion I found a vintage Beatles Vanity set and a large Beatles Drum alarm clock which cost £25 – much more than I would normally spend but it paid off as they made £200 on eBay. To me, it's about spotting something that really epitomises an era or a bygone time that people look back on as a halcyon period. The items I bought I thought would appeal to those who remember playing with Sindy dolls, or who were into the Beatles, and I knew someone somewhere would want to relive these memories and purchase these pieces.

Nursery sets featuring Winnie the Pooh, Basil Brush, Beatrix Potter, etc are well worth buying if not for your own collection then to sell on. Anything that typifies an era, for example 1950s curtains, 1970s fondue sets – all have their own market for collectors so if the price is right the return you can make by selling such items to collectors is well worthwhile. Nowadays it's not just the classic toys that can make money. Think of the advances in electronics and communications. An original 1980s mobile phone, a 1970s LED watch or calculator and the early Sega games all have collectability, particularly among the Japanese, and selling this sort of item on eBay could not be easier, particularly if you've picked them up for a song at a boot sale.

In 2002 a Sony TR-55 transistor radio was listed on eBay with the opening bid of $10. The radio was made by electronics giant Tokyo Tsushin Kogyo Ltd and this particular radio was one of the relatively few known to have survived. Historically important because it was the world's first electronic portable, pocket-sized radio to be built entirely by one company from the inside out, the radio was described as in good condition despite not actually working and it sold for $11,100.

Top tip: **Even if you're not into toys, there are plenty of new toys around at boot sales worth buying for all sorts of reasons. Many people collect good toys to take to local hospital children's wards or for local charity shops to resell. It's a fun way of doing something for a good cause. So-called DINKY (dual-income-no-kids-yet) couples should certainly buy up a selection of nearly new toys, put them in a box and save them for when friends with young children visit. It keeps the children amused for hours, out of your hair and scores plenty of Brownie points on the favourite uncle scoreboard.**

CLOTHING

The huge trend for 'vintage' clothing should not be overlooked. With high-street chains such as Oasis launching their own 'new' vintage, clothes styled on vintage designs, there is incredible demand on eBay for true vintage pieces. I bought three

INXS t-shirts from a boot sale for £1.50 and sold them on eBay for £12 each, for example. I have never managed to get hold of any vintage 1970s punk Vivienne Westwood items, which would be a great buy. Lee and Eileen Hopkinson from Essex saw their collection of old punk clothing, which had been kept at the back of their wardrobe for years, realise £8,000 at Sotheby's Passion for Fashion sale four years ago. A pair of Spiderman bondage boots bought by Lee Hopkinson in 1976 for £50, the equivalent of two weeks' wages, made £660.

If you do spot or find a stall which has interesting items it's always worth asking whether the seller has other examples that are either still in their car or perhaps languishing at home. Sellers will often be limited by car space as to what they can actually take to a car boot sale so if it's records you are after, for example, it's always worth asking stallholders whether they have any records for sale even if you cannot see any on the stall at that moment.

Moving Markets

Over the time that I have been going to boot sales the demand for different sorts of items has changed dramatically. A decade ago, Carlton ware china was in high demand and I remember hearing of someone who had purchased an entire tea service at a boot sale for £5, which was worth £500. Since then, with the onset of eBay, many more people are aware of the potential value of items. This has meant that many people ask the top price for items at boot sales, but on the other hand it can mean that the prices have come down because there is now a worldwide market and a worldwide availability – at a price – for just about anything through eBay. Similarly, kitchenalia such as TG Green could still be snapped up for £1–£2 a pot compared to £40 today. As for 1950s glass fish – well I actually witnessed dealers smashing them up at the end of a boot sale when they hadn't sold for a couple of pounds but today the general asking price starts at £15 and can be as much as £40 for a good example. Clearly, it's important to keep ahead of the market developments and eBay is a fabulous source of prices paid and prices being asked. My entire collection of Kleenware green and white striped kitchen storage pots cost no more than £50 in total and I have nearly sixty pieces. To replace these today would set me back around £3,000 – such has the market changed and the demand for kitchenalia increased.

My entire collection of sixty Kleenware pieces cost £50 and if I were to replace them now it would set me back £3,000.

Much of this shift can be spotted at boot sales first. Auction houses tend to be the last to reflect any ongoing change. I can remember just four years ago asking Christie's whether they would consider selling *Star Wars* collectables and the answer was an emphatic 'No'. Yet I was recently at Weller's auction in Chertsey in Surrey filming for *Cash in the Attic* where a collection of 150 mint and boxed *Star Wars* figurines sold for £8,000. It's not a case of whether or not the collection was actually worth £8,000 – the point is that there are collectors out there to whom the collection is worth £8,000 and there is increasing demand and competition among them to secure the best and rarest pieces – whatever the cost.

A collection of boxed original *Star Wars* figures in mint condition recently sold for £8,000.

When I first started going to boot sales it was possible to buy a good clean example of a classic 1960s Roberts Radio for £3. Since then the price has risen to at least £20 and of course

Roberts as a company has ridden the retro trend by launching its Roberts Revival range. The classic Roberts radios are now being made again in a range of colours and retailing for at least £100. Frankly, it was a lot more fun buying a vintage example for £3 than it can possibly be parting with £100 for an identical example made yesterday. The price of the originals may have risen considerably but they are still a bargain compared with the new versions!

Top tip: Keep on top of what is selling and making good money by making friends with dealers and traders at antiques fairs and boot sales, checking eBay and the www.antiquestradegazette.com website at least once a week. The latter gives a weekly round-up of news from auction houses across the country. The site has a search engine that allows you to type in an item you may have found, e.g. teddy bear, and bring up stories and results for teddy bears from auction houses. Your example may not be there but it's a good starting point for identifying possible manufacturers and the age of the item.

What Not to Buy

Soft toys for children that are anything other than new, in case they are not appropriate for today's safety standards.

Items where the batteries have leaked, as this makes them virtually irreparable.

Electrical items, unless you are happy you have a qualified electrician in the neighbourhood who can rewire it safely for you and thus ensure that it is not going to be a dangerous device.

Baby equipment including pushchairs, prams, and in particular car seats. These are often hardly used and look like great bargains, but there is no warranty or guarantee that they still meet safety requirements. When it comes to children, life is too precious to take any risks – so only buy such items new from proper retail outlets.

Items that are rusted up, unless there is some practical or aesthetic reason. Removing rust is not only virtually impossible but also a specialist job, and should not be attempted by amateurs.

Items that are clearly not with their rightful owners. I know someone who bought a lawnmower with SCC on the side from a boot sale only to discover later that SCC stood for Southend County Council. If you suspect an item is stolen but have no direct proof you should bring your concerns to the attention of the boot sale organiser rather than the stallholder, who, if legitimate, could have a legal case against you for making false accusations. Similarly, if you buy something you suspect is stolen you are in effect handling stolen goods and this is a criminal offence.

Make-up, detergents or perfume unless unopened, as they could pose hygiene and health problems. In some cases, of course, people purchase perfume for the bottle itself, in which case it should be emptied and cleaned as soon as possible.

Anything that could be deemed an offensive or dangerous weapon, including knives of any kind, although most boot sale organisers ensure that such items cannot be sold.

Real fur or leather, unless you are prepared to pay the hefty dry cleaning and specialist cleaning costs. Items such as this that have not been stored or looked after properly can be unhygienic.

Computers or mobile phones that are not from regular or recommended dealers, as there is no guarantee that these items will work or are legitimately sold, unless you are a computer genius able to build up a computer from scratch if there is any problem.

How to Haggle

Don't cut off your nose to spite your face when it comes to haggling. In August 2003 Lawrence's auction house in Crewkerne sold a William de Morgan charger featuring a design of stylised swans and a galleon for £3,000. It had been bought at a local boot sale for £10. Now £10 might sound like a lot of money for a large plate, but clearly the buyer knew what he was looking at and must have realised this was going to be his bargain of a lifetime. There would have been no point in trying to haggle the price down from £10 and risk losing the piece for the sake of a couple of pounds. Once you've spotted something you want, it's part of the whole boot sale ethos to haggle for the best price. Manners maketh the man or woman and the best approach is polite and friendly – remember that the person selling has no obligation to sell to you and can even opt not to part with a piece. I have seen this happen when people have been too aggressive in their haggling. Obviously, your opening shot is to establish the price the seller is looking for, so here are some suggestions:

If the seller sticks to his or her price and will not budge, don't get the hump. Simply weigh up whether you feel the item is at a good price or not and make a decision either to purchase it or move on. If you move on, however, don't expect the item to be there when you have second thoughts and return.

If you have a price in mind that you are prepared to pay, for example £10, have the £10 note in your hand – it can make a huge psychological difference to people to actually see the money there ready for the taking rather than to be simply talking figures in the air. Someone asking £11 for an item is more likely to accept £10 if he or she can see the note there crisp and ready to be handed over.

Remember that, unfortunately, boot sales have in the past been easy targets for people passing counterfeit money and therefore many sellers will be loath to change up or accept large notes, particularly £50 notes. These are rarely in general circulation and therefore most people would not know a genuine one from a fake one. The seller has the right to refuse a sale and your money if he or she so chooses.

Some sellers will not give a set price but simply ask the buyer to make an offer. This can be difficult. I have seen sellers withdraw items if the offer has been much more than they had expected. The seller then gets nervous that the item really has great worth and decides not to sell it but to take it to a specialist instead. However, making a ridiculously low offer can offend, so honesty is the best policy. If it is a piece that you have been seeking for a long time, let the seller know your motivation for buying it and explain why it is worth something to you, but unlikely to be of interest to every boot sale visitor. On the other hand, if you do manage to secure what you deem to be the bargain of the year, do not rub the seller's face in it. I know a boot sale organiser who banned one man from his sites after the buyer purchased a diamond ring from a lady seller for £5 and then promptly told her it was diamond and worth at least £1,000. Hardly necessary and arguably rather underhand.

I really don't recommend underhand tactics such as using children to barter at stalls on your behalf. Getting them to negotiate the price on McDonalds toys that are missing from their collections is one thing; getting them to haggle on the price of a silver mirror, saying that they have to have it to go with their Barbie doll, is unlikely to work and may well set the seller against you.

Be truthful about your spending levels wherever possible. I have seen many people haggle and haggle over the odd 50p on the basis that it is the last 50p they have and they cannot manage a full £1 – only to pull at £5 note out of their pocket when the deal is struck. What's the point? All that happens is that the seller is left to feel a fool and you come across as the twenty-first-century version of Scrooge.

On a point of principle I will not haggle with sellers who are stalling out on behalf of charities. Often this is in an unofficial capacity but with the best of intentions. In Essex, several of the amateur animal rescue centres have free stalls at boot sales so they can sell donated items and raise funds for the excellent work they do – haggling here can quite literally mean the difference between abandoned puppies being cared for or dying.

Top tip: If you have spotted one item you like on a stall, tell the stallholder you want that piece and ask if they can hold onto it while you just check there's nothing else on the same stall you are interested in. There may be several items of interest and this way you can select everything, put it together, and negotiate an overall price for the lot with the aim of getting a greater discount as you are buying more than one item.

Scratchers

A decade ago a lady who had cleared out a neighbour's house after her death decided to retrieve a teddy bear that she had put in a bin bag. Christie's auctioneers, who later sold the bear, explained, 'It seems that although the bear had been thrown out with the rest of the rubbish, it played on the lady's mind and so she went back into the bins to get it.' Good job too, as this bear was in fact one of 600 Black Steiff bears made for Great Britain to commemorate tragic sinking of the *Titanic* on 14 April 1912. Despite a £8,000–£10,000 estimate it sold for £22,000. Even this price appears a bargain considering that by December 2000 a similar example of a Black Steiff sold for £91,750.

It's not unusual to see people poking around the skips and bins at the end of a boot sale checking for any left-behind items that take their eye. I was amazed when we were filming at the RNLI charity boot sale at Henley-on-Thames to see no fewer than twenty very well-dressed people climbing into the skip parked right at the front entrance as boot sale buyers and sellers were packing up for the day. My surprise was simply to see such activity in what is thought to be such a posh place, given that these people are often rather derogatorily referred to as 'scratchers'. My son has had the benefit of some really wonderful books that had just been dumped into rubbish bins at the end of the day – something which, to me, as a book lover, is total sacrilege anyway.

Do bear in mind that the law comes into effect when it comes to searching skips, rubbish bins and items located on other people's land. To some extent there is an argument that items left in skips or bins are in effect abandoned or dumped by the original owner. However, there is also an argument that the items then become the property of the person who owns the skip or bin or on whose land the skip or bin is located. It might sound pedantic, and it is a pretty hard rule to enforce, but the way round it is to always check with the boot sale organisers *before* diving into their skips and bins. Generally speaking, most organisers turn a blind eye on the basis that there will be a bit less rubbish for them to clear up.

Top tip: Never be too proud to ask and rummage around a skip or bin. In 2001 Phillips auctioneers (as it was before being taken over by Bonhams) sold a ceramic mouse study which was found on an old rubbish heap; it realised £1,600. It was a George Tinworth Royal Doulton Lambethware group called 'The Combat' and had survived in perfect condition. In August

2002 Christie's Fine Toys, Trains and Toy Soldiers auction included a collection of *Thunderbirds* models saved from a trip to the rubbish dump some thirty years before and the cache of twenty-three items realised £112,863, with the top price being the £37,600 paid for a John Tracy head.

Conclusion

- The early bird catches the worm, as Margaret Simms proved. After weeks of turning up at her local Manchester boot sale at 5 a.m. she spotted a Clarice Cliff charger, which she bought for £1. She is now celebrating her windfall with a holiday in Bulgaria after the charger sold at Christie's for £1,976.

- Don't be too proud to haggle on prices, particularly at the end of the day when most people want to get rid of the rest of their stuff and go home.

- Don't cut off your nose to spite your face – if you spot the bargain of the year or simply something that you really love, don't lose it because you won't pay the seller's asking price.

- Wear comfortable shoes, plenty of layers and remember sun screen in the summer. Take plenty of change and a rucksack for your finds so your hands are free to rummage around the stalls.

- Be prepared to go to plenty of boot sales on a regular basis as they can change from week to week depending on who is there selling.

CHAPTER FIVE

VALUATION VIRGINS!

The popularity of the programmes I present, including *Boot Sale Challenge*, *Car Booty* and *Cash in the Attic*, is due to a combination of everyone hoping they have something of value and realising this value. For those who apply to take part on the programmes and get through – there are thousands of applications received every week – it can be a double-edged sword. Very often the pieces that have been treasured are not the most valuable, but a neglected or disliked piece can be valued at a price that is surprising. Two years ago, when Bonhams specialist John Kelly was called to a house in the West Country to value some silver and jewellery he also found a clock, which the vendor described as 'hideous', hidden under a towel. It had been purchased for £1.50 at a boot sale ten years previously and was a large Archibald Knox for Liberty of London wall clock made of pewter featuring cabochons. It made £5,975 at

Bonhams Arts and Crafts sale later that year.

The world in which I work is full of stories such as this, amazing coincidences with mythical results and it's this very unpredictability that makes my job and that of auctioneers, collectors and dealers so exciting. What everyone wants to avoid, of course, is underselling an item or throwing something away that just could be worth a fortune. The only way to ensure this doesn't happen is to get items properly valued and this in turn requires considerable time, effort, imagination, resourcefulness and perseverance.

Initial Information

Most people are now aware of Internet search engines such as Google, which can help give useful websites, articles and information on eras and areas of collectability. However, few people realise that by taking their piece to any auction house across the country they can ask for it to be valued and get advice from the auction house. This gives the collector a firm idea of whether the piece has a value worth investigating further or whether it is simply of 'decorative value', a term often used to imply that while attractive there's no underlying value to the piece. Similarly, many dealers and collectors will be happy to help point you in the right direction and eBay itself is a great reference source for information and potential valuations. So if you've got a hunch that the boot sale bargain buy you made just might be worth considerably more than you paid for it, here's what to do:

Check www.google.co.uk. Try several searches of the item you have, e.g: Merrythought Teddy Bear – Merrythought Ltd – Teddy Bears – Teddy Bear auction – Teddy Bear clubs.

Check www.ebay.com. Try several searches of the item under: toy listings, completed items, powersellers and shops. Typing 'Merrythought Teddy Bear' in the search engine will get you every such example, new and old, listed and being sold at that time starting with the auction of a 'Merrythought Teddy Bear' that is the first to end. By scrolling down the page and onto 'completed items' you will call up a list of Merrythought Teddy Bears which have been sold recently, with options to retrieve sales from the past day, past seven days or sometimes longer. This latter option will give you actual hammer prices paid, whereas the current listings do not feature completed or actual results. Most sellers know to include a photograph too so it can help identify your particular Merrythought Teddy Bear, e.g. it may become apparent from eBay listings that your teddy bear is a limited edition or a 1960s Cheeky Bear and thus you can start refining your search on www.google.co.uk and elsewhere with 'Merrythought Cheeky Teddy Bear 1960s'.

Check the Internet for collectors' club websites. Companies such as Merrythought Ltd have their own registered websites, in this case at www.merrythought.co.uk, and there are email contacts on such sites along with contact details, addresses, links and phone numbers that will be useful. There are also collectors' clubs, retailers and enthusiasts who have their own websites. In the case of 'Merrythought Teddy Bear' you are likely to call up www.teddybears.co.uk which is the site of teddy bear retailer Ian Pout of Teddy Bears of Witney and

Sue Pearson's site for her shop in Brighton, Sussex, or Bears 'n' Bunnies at Bluewater in Kent. Now you are starting to get some specialist contacts in the field, who may well be able to help you with valuations and more information on your particular 'Merrythought Teddy Bear'.

Check www.bbc.co.uk/antiques. This is an amazingly extensive website containing all sorts of articles about antiques and collectables and other finds from various shows. It features several stories about Merrythought Teddy Bears discovered on the *Antiques Roadshow* and also gives useful information on other contacts, along with the opportunity to contact fellow enthusiasts on the website's message board – although frustratingly this is both vetted and closed at night.

Check www.vam.ac.uk. This is the website for both the Victoria and Albert Museum in London and its sister museum, the Bethnal Green Toy Museum in East London. It's an amazing treasure trove of photographs and information, which can take some time to access depending on your computer capacity. I often find it easier to actually visit the museum itself, use its internal website computers, which are free to all and email myself the information and photographs to my home computer. Similarly, a search on www.google.co.uk of 'Teddy Bear Museum' will help bring up further professional and amateur museums which may be able to offer help and advice.

Check www.antiquestradegazette.com. I love this site because, although it is massively and often rather snootily opinionated, it has great editorial coverage of auctions, forthcoming auctions, auction results and other really interesting trade news, including details of stolen items and long-lost pieces that have been recently rediscovered. It can be hard to work round and it takes a long time to upload the information after you have registered but it's worth persevering if you'd rather do this than invest £74 a year in a subscription. Personally, I like having the paper copy to keep me up to date and I use the search engine on the news section for past stories of interest and background research. Obviously, if you type in 'Merrythought Teddy Bear' under the auction results heading you will get a list of auction prices realised for such bears and many of these will have photos with them too.

Top tip: Always have a pen and paper handy for these searches. They will often throw up further websites, links or contacts that might prove useful but are better jotted down for further reference or new searches – it's all too easy to get distracted by clicking through links to other sites, then clicking 'back' to find the original site you were on, only to realise that in the meantime your computer has gone offline or five hours of your life have just passed you by.

Preparing for a Valuation

Once you have some initial information on the article you will probably be interested in learning more about its potential value, so the next stage is:

Photograph the item from several angles, against a plain white or cream background and in a good strong light so the photograph will reflect the item's true colours, condition and design. Make sure that any identification marks, stamps or manufacturers' names and/or numbers are photographed separately and included because numbers generally indicate either the year of production, the design shape or registration number, while initials can help further identify a designer, painter or modeller.

Top tip: The advance of the Internet, digital photography and email capacity means that many auction houses and dealers can now accept digital images and this will at least help them to get a general idea of the item you possess. Some dealers may also consider allowing you to send mobile-phone camera photos, although bear in mind that many of these images are extremely small and may make full identification and therefore valuation difficult. Additionally, sending mobile-phone pictures usually involves a separate charge for both the sender and the recipient, which can be extremely expensive so check before you send.

<u>Make a note of the history</u>, known provenance and measurements of the item, i.e. it was purchased from an individual who claimed it had been in the family for at least fifty years, or it was purchased from an individual who had been given the toy as a child. Measurements are important because it's very hard to tell the actual size of something from a photograph alone.

> *Top tip:* Include any information that you yourself have been able to find from Internet searches or other friends, collectors and dealers but be prepared to accept that a specialist may not agree with the information or valuation you have. A general opinion is not the same as specialist advice.

Be honest about the condition of the piece, making a note of any cracks, splits, missing pieces, restoration or repair that you are aware of. Include any past valuation information that you have, including valuations received for insurance purposes as this will all help towards an up-to-date valuation.

> *Top tip:* Making a claim for an 'accident' to a valued item under your household insurance if the article was already damaged or broken counts as fraud and is a criminal offence. Insurance companies are increasingly refusing to pay out for items that have not previously been brought to their attention within your household contents policy and will most definitely insist on actual proof of damage. (For more on insuring items and claiming on insurance, see page 244 onwards.)

Choosing the Type of Valuation

This is quite exacting if it is for insurance purposes and is to be effective and accepted by an insurance company. Bonhams, Sotheby's and Christie's all have valuation departments with specialists covering probate or estate valuations and insurance valuations. Prices for an expert to visit a collector's home, assess a collection and provide a written report start at around £500 a day. Even here, there's no such thing as a straightforward insurance valuation. One auctioneer I spoke to explained:

> People tend to be very vague about the purpose of their valuation. It's vital they decide whether the valuation is for insurance, insurance at replacement or in the light of assessing assets for probate. If they simply want their collection checked out with a view to selling it at auction that is usually free after initial consultations with department specialists. For an official insurance valuation, fees vary depending on where a collector is in the country but within London it's about £100 per hour. For that you get two bound copies of the valuation with items listed and valued, and an index summarising each category; photographs can be incorporated for an additional charge.

Top tip: Despite the level of skill and expertise the top four London auction houses have at hand, even this may not be enough to satisfy insurance firms. Most insurers still insist on visiting and assessing collections via their own surveyors and experts.

You have to remember that you are asking people to help you here and you will be hoping to tap into their specialist knowledge. In most fields of life, using a specialist involves a fee. A car mechanic, electrician, plumber, teacher, dentist or doctor will all charge for their specialist advice even if it is via the

NHS. The least you should do is to remember that no one *has* to help and that courtesy, good manners, a 'please' and a 'thank you' go a long way.

> *Top tip:* **Bonhams' Head of Twentieth-century Decorative Arts, Mark Oliver, says:**
>
> Most auction houses will provide a valuation for auction purposes free of charge, either by the collector sending in a photo or bringing the piece in to the auction house. I give values for auction which means having the knowledge and expertise to know what the piece will sell for on the secondary market, but it's not an exact science, more intelligent guesswork. Photos are usually enough for an auction valuation, but you couldn't do a proper insurance valuation this way. That's where the actual valuation department comes in.

VALUATION FOR SELLING

Sotheby's explains, 'We will visit houses to value and send in specialists as required. You can't beat an expert with their hands on an object valuing an item via their expertise and knowledge. We work on a flat-fee basis but that's negotiable and we're more competitive than the majority of other auctioneers. If we want to do something then we can charge a lower fee to get the work because we're a large enough company to take that cost.'

It's an approach that has paid Sotheby's dividends. Called in to undertake a probate valuation and estate sale for Benacre

Hall near Lowestoft in Suffolk the general valuers spotted a painting of interest. Drawing on the Old Master experts within Sotheby's, the painting was finally found to be a thirteenth-century work called *The Madonna and Child Enthroned with Angels* by the Italian master Cimabue. The painting sold four years ago for £2m.

> *Top tip:* If you are considering selling several items at once, whether these are general or specialist, it's worth enquiring about selling everything through one auction house in order to haggle on the commission and charges that you will pay. Remember, if you don't ask for a discount you won't get one anyway so you've nothing to lose by asking whether it's possible to 'discount' the overall cost of the fees. Not every auction house will do this, of course, and the discount will depend on the potential total value of the collection or collectables you are selling.

Selling via a Traditional Auction

Before you sell anything at auction you will need to have it valued. The value of the piece will make a difference as to where you are most likely to want to sell it. Items worth £500–£1,000 may be best placed in a specialist London auction house sale where maximum publicity can be achieved but the cost of selling the item can be much higher than at a regional sale room. Lower-cost items may be best sold at local auction houses, which can be conveniently accessed and may well have lower charges, helping you to maximise the money you make.

Clearly, a valuation for insurance purposes or with a view to selling requires considerable work and investment of both time and money. For items that are likely to be worth £100 or less, or for items that are of interest only or 'decorative value' (in other words sentimental value rather than hard cash) there are still plenty of resources available that can help, including:

Contact auction houses in your local region, including regional branches of the larger auction houses such as Christie's, Sotheby's and Bonhams. These are listed on their main websites at www.christies.com, www.sothebys.com and www.bonhams.com. Others nearer your locality can be found in the *Yellow Pages* under 'Auctioneers' or in your local newspapers. Ask for the auction house's opening times, location and whether they have a specialist department that deals in, for example, paintings, toys or silver. If they have, take your item to that specialist department and if not, move on until you find an auction house that does have a specialist.

Top tip: Ask the auction house if it is a member of the ISVA – The Incorporated Society of Valuers and Auctioneers – or any alternative professional body. If they are not, it's best to try another auction room that has taken the necessary steps to register with a professional body. Most reputable auction houses will allow you to take the item in, or post in a photograph (non-returnable), and get a free word-of-mouth valuation. Remember, though, that this is unlikely to satisfy insurers and you may well have a wait depending on how fast auction houses can or cannot process such requests. These are businesses and their prime purpose is to concentrate on their core moneymaking venture, which is selling at their own regular auctions rather than offering free valuations.

Ask for the auction house specialist likely to cover the era or area that your item falls under. You may need to make an appointment – all auction houses give free valuations to those who go in with their pieces seeking a valuation. If an auction house tries to charge for a verbal valuation then go elsewhere, but remember that if you are asking for a valuation for insurance purposes there will be a charge both from dealers, specialists and auction houses.

Top tip: Consider a special trip to London where you can visit Bonhams, Sotheby's and Christie's front desks. Here you can present your item and request that a member of staff from the relevant department give you a valuation. This is a free service and very much underused by collectors. For a quick trip to the City, you are assured of a true and accurate valuation which may be a delight or a disappointment – but at least you finally know the significance of your cherished collectable.

Online valuations. Given the success of the *Antiques Roadshow*, *Cash in the Attic*, *Flog It!* and *Car Booty*, all of which owe a great deal of their popularity to people's thirst for valuations, it's surprising that there is not a proper, cost-effective online valuation service available. Unfortunately, it seems that many people are unwilling to pay for such a service, even though it could be money well spent and prevent someone from under-pricing an item. Four years ago QXL.com hired the *Antiques Roadshow's* one-time presenter Hugh Scully to launch just such a service. The idea was that this would be manned by experienced and vetted valuers, and collectors could get their item properly valued for a £12 fee. However, the big hiccup at the time was that a digital image of the piece to be valued had to be submitted and few people at that time had access to or owned a digital camera. So perhaps there is still a gap in the market for this sort of service but, of course, it will only work if people are prepared to pay for it and I have a hunch that few are.

Books and launches. Whenever experts or presenters launch books there is usually the opportunity to get a free valuation at a book signing or launch up and down the country. When a book is launched there is a promotional tour of some description, which involves radio and press interviews regionally and appearances at local bookshops. Always check with the bookshop beforehand but it should usually be possible to get a quick valuation or advice on the day.

Auction house valuation days around the country. These are occasionally advertised in the local papers and may involve the London auction houses visiting the regions and having an 'Open Day' event where items can be valued. Alternatively, local auction houses may host open days themselves. Either way, it's a great free service and one that is worth using. Remember, from the auction house's point of view, time is being invested in free valuations on the basis that for all this effort one or two nice pieces may turn up. The chances are that most vendors – once they are told a piece has an unexpected high value – are happy to sell. Therefore, the auction house hosting the valuation day is the one most likely to get the piece for inclusion in one of its sales. This is how things work and it will not affect the valuation you get – but do not feel under pressure to offer up a treasured piece if you do not want to sell it. There is no obligation for you to sell, and you can always take the person or auction house's contact details and get in touch at a later date should you decide to sell in the future.

Antiques fairs. Dealers have hundreds and thousands of stories about 'punters' or members of the public who pass their stall pontificating about the charges levied for items on their stalls. 'My grandmother had one of those but she threw it out, how much is it?' is a classic question bandied around antiques fairs by members of the public who are simply interested in long-lost treasure rather than purchasing items at the fair. It's a fine line between showing an interest in a piece and getting a valuation from a dealer. Many dealers are very against valuing items at antiques fairs – while they are valuing a piece for free, a customer may be walking past who might otherwise have bought a piece from the dealer's stall. Not only that, but it takes years to learn about the business so it takes a lot for them to share their knowledge with you for nothing. Having said this, there are also plenty of dealers who love helping collectors out. Some take the long-term view that if you are interested now you may turn into a future buyer; others simply enjoy the whole community spirit of antiques fairs and will happily chat and exchange views and information with anyone. The key is to ask a dealer who is selling items similar to the one you have, whether or not he could help you with some advice on getting the item valued – just be prepared for a 'No' and be pleasantly gracious for a 'Yes'.

Avoid 'knockers'. These are unscrupulous dealers who go around neighbourhoods knocking on people's doors asking if they have anything they would be prepared to sell. Obviously, it's never advisable to let such people in unless you have made an appointment and asked them to visit your home. No matter what they offer, suggest, advise, or how nice they seem, there is no excuse for attempting to trade this way and reputable dealers advise the same thing – leave the door firmly closed. Similarly, anyone leafleting an area offering to visit and value items should be carefully checked out before being invited in. Local community police will have further advice on this, but if – as has happened recently where I live – your area has been leafleted by someone using only a mobile telephone number as a contact, or a number that is clearly outside of the area, be very careful. The local auction house or antiques dealer trading from an established venue is much more advisable than a leafleter who could quite simply be scamming an area and who will be impossible to locate after the event.

By now you may be so attached to your bargain buy that you want it to have pride of place in your home or, if the piece is worth under £100, you find it's more profitable to take a chance selling it on eBay (see Chapter Six). However, if your item is large, particularly specialist or has excited the valuer into a frenzy because it is a rarity of great value, then it's worth looking at selling it. Obviously, I'm concentrating on selling items on eBay which is the best way for most people to create businesses, offload unwanted clutter or generally find a useful extra or main source of income. However, I should point out, with my cynical journalist's hat on, that eBay is very good at promoting itself – usually in conjunction with the *Sun* newspaper. The record-breaking Levi jeans that sold on eBay, and Prime Minister's wife Cherie Blair's purchase of an alarm clock for son Leo and a pair of pink shoes for herself have all found their way into the headlines of the tabloid press. Yes, it's interesting but it's not really news. Furthermore, always ask yourself who exactly has bought all these weird and wonderful items for such headline-making prices. Let's consider the possibility that eBay for all its greatness isn't necessarily always the answer. Bonhams' Mark Oliver makes the point – and yes he may be biased working for a traditional auction house, but the facts and figures speak for themselves: 'In our last Doulton sale of 2000 we had a Royal Doulton Toby jug that had twice been on an Internet auction and failed to meet its £1,200 reserve. The vendor then brought the piece to us and we sold it for £5,000, which I am sure was due to the fact that the interested parties could actually view and handle the piece ahead of bidding, which is something that will never be possible on the Internet.' So, while selling on eBay is covered in Chapter Six, let's also consider the other routes to making money and finding a fortune.

Selling at a specialist auction

This can be advantageous, but remember these are likely to be held once or twice a year at most. For example, BBR Auctions of Elsecar in Yorkshire hold specialist Advertising, Royal Doulton and kitchenalia sales but the kitchenalia sales take place only twice a year. Therefore, if you miss one of these sales, you have a long wait before your kitchenalia can be entered into the next specialist sale and even longer to wait until the money comes through from the auction itself.

Visit the auctioneers

See how popular one of their sales is before deciding whether or not to sell there. If the sales are not well attended, you know it is unlikely that people will bid high prices for your items. Remember your discussions with an auction house, and indeed your decision to sell through them, remain confidential between yourself and the auction house. This is auction etiquette and accepted within the trade.

Take advice and be realistic about the price

If the value of your piece is £50, anything at auction from £35–£65 is a reasonable sum to expect. Don't submit the piece with an unrealistic £200 'reserve' or it will never sell.

Auctioneers will be able to give you an idea of what price to expect and advise you on the reserve – the bottom price at which the item can be sold.

Consider whether or not to have a reserve price

If you are not bothered about the price made, then consider selling the item clearly marked in the catalogue as 'without reserve', which encourages people to believe that they can get it at bargain price. Some of the best auction 'surprises' are a result of items being marked 'without reserve'. Two collectors decide that they will bid on the piece, get auction fever and end up sending the price rocketing. If you have an idea in your mind of the price you want and the auctioneer believes this to be realistic then you should set a reserve price with the auctioneer. This will mean that the item cannot be sold for a ridiculously low figure but the reserve price will be kept from bidders in line with auctioneer/vendor confidentiality.

Check auctioneer's discretion

Most auction houses reserve the right to sell something at their 'discretion'. This may be 10–20% around the estimate or reserve. In other words, if your item is estimated to sell at £60–£100 and you have a £60 reserve on the piece, you need to ask what the auctioneer's discretion is. If it is 10% this will allow the auctioneer to sell the item for £54 hammer price. This is £6 under your reserve price, but within 10% of the reserve price. Most auctioneers will explain this to you further and will ensure that the reserve price, i.e. £60, is absolute if this is what you require.

Will the catalogue do the item justice?

There is often a cost involved in featuring an item or piece with a full-colour photograph within an auction catalogue. The London auction houses can charge upwards of £500 to 'feature' an item in colour within one of its catalogues, which means it's only worthwhile if the article is of substantial value. However, Bonhams is quite good at photographing several lots together within a catalogue and this helps to reduce the overall fee. It's also vital nowadays that the full catalogue including photographs is available online with plenty of time to allow online bidders to decide whether or not to view in person, bid on commission or bid online. Clearly you will need to check the charges but do bear in mind that it can be well worth investing some money in advance to ensure that the item is well presented – after all, a picture can be worth a thousand words.

Will the catalogue description be sent to you?

Most auction houses will ask their vendors to check the item's description to make sure that they are happy with the layout and the details included and then ask them to sign this off and return a copy of the description. It is at this point that you are unlikely to be able to withdraw the piece if you change your mind about selling and you should not consider objecting to the description unless it is clearly wrong. Do check that the estimate is what has been agreed.

Ask about publicity

Some auction houses have much better relationships with local and national newspapers than others. Henry Aldridge & Son Auctioneers, for example, has an excellent relationship with the tabloid press and has had several of its lots, ranging from a *Titanic* deckchair which made £33,500 to the world's earliest known Christmas card which made £22,350, featured in the national papers. Creating such interest can make all the

Henry Aldridge & Son Auctioneers sold a *Titanic* deckchair for £33,500 and the world's earliest Christmas card made £22,350.

difference to the attendance at a sale and the bidding and therefore the end result. The more publicity the better. When I was writing a week-ly collectables column for the *Mail on Sunday*, a young man walked into Christie's regional office in Yorkshire with a Mickey Mouse toy from the 1930s. He had brought it down from his grandfather's loft after seeing my column about a similar item – unsure whether it had a value, he was delighted when it went on to set a world record for a Disney toy, selling for more than £10,000.

Remember that this is not a free service

The seller as well as the buyer pays commission; that's how auctioneers make their money. The seller can expect to pay between 10% and 20% of the final hammer price back to the auctioneer. So if an item sells for £100, the buyer of that piece will pay £110 at 10% commission and the seller can expect back £90, the £100 hammer price minus 10% commission. Some auctioneers also charge a 'lot fee' of at least £2 per item listed in the auction, so ask if this is the case. If you have several pieces to submit, it may be better to put them in a large 'group' lot so you only pay the lot fee once. Remember too that the auction house pays Value Added Tax on the commission that it charges you, both as a buyer and a seller. So if your overall bill for selling £1,000-worth of items is £100 commission (i.e. 10% commission charges), there will be VAT to pay on the £100 commission. As VAT is charged by the Government at 17.5% this will be a further £17.50 to pay, taking the total bill to £117.50 which will be deducted from the £1,000 worth of items that have been sold. VAT can be reclaimed in certain cases (see Chapter Eight).

If the item is unsold

If the item does not sell, you will only be charged the lot fee – if applicable and the pieces will be returned to you. You will have to pick them up though.

If the item does sell, the money will be paid to you, usually by cheque within four to six weeks. Some local auction houses will pay out in cash within the week, but you need to check each individual auction house's system.

SELLING TO DEALERS

Dealers have spent their lives acquiring information and learning their trade – most will tell you that their biggest lessons have been learnt through mistakes made. As a result, they are astute buyers who will not offer you the full retail value of your piece. This is not a conspiracy – you have to remember that dealers spend days travelling the country, attending auctions, and standing out in the pouring rain at antiques fairs to earn a living. They may well be interested in the item that you have to sell, but they will be looking to pay anything from 50%–75% of the item's value as they will then have to find a buyer for the piece and make money themselves on the original purchase price. Ask around for reputable dealers from other contacts you've made; you cannot beat a personal recommendation. This route arguably requires more work on your behalf and will not be as anonymous a sale as the auction house or Internet auction route.

SELLING VIA A TRADITIONAL ANTIQUES FAIR

You can always consider taking a stand at an antiques fair yourself, but be warned, it's hard work, an early start and brings no guarantee of a sale. BBR's auctioneer Alan Blakeman highlights the point, 'We sold a collection of seven jugs advertising various drinks, which a gentleman had bought from a pub clear-out. Some years later he took a stand at a local antiques fair and tried to sell them, charging £150 for the three he liked best and £45 for the others. None of them sold, but we managed to sell the collection two years ago for £8,000 in total.' Alternatively, you can simply attend a fair and see if you can get a dealer to make you an offer – it's not as involved as standing at the fair itself, but it's just as much work. Three years ago, I made my usual trip to Newark Antiques Fair, which is held every other month at Newark in Nottinghamshire. It's a great venue for anyone interested in interior design, collectables, antiques or just seeing how the true antiques trade really works. After all, in 2001 a dealer at Newark managed to find a copper master etching plate for £25 and this later sold for £22,000. Anyway, I went with the express purpose of seeing just how hard or easy it could be to make money from items that I had bought in the past. I had three items with me and this is what happened:

A Ladybird children's shop display house, purchased at the same antique fair the year before for £35, was offered to Lisa Silver, who runs the Tin Shop and is a regular trader at Newark. Lisa is the sort of dealer who is a pleasure to deal with. Friendly, helpful, but not pushy, she is a source of infinite knowledge and instantly recognised the piece I had bought on a hunch: 'It's 1960s and would have been a shop display piece. I have seen examples before but I have to say they have been cardboard versions while this is a cast piece which actually makes it rarer. Unfortunately, it's rather large and while I have no doubt that I'd sell it eventually, it's not a quick turnover item – more a case of taking it and waiting for the right person to come into the shop to buy it, which could be a week or a year.'

Lisa explained that the key for any dealer is having a buyer lined up for a piece. This means that the items are not simply sitting on the shelf but are quickly moved on, thus turning a profit. More importantly, she adds, 'In the case of the Ladybird house it's got potential because not only is it an advertising piece but it will attract collectors of Ladybird and children's items. I would expect it to sell for anything between £125–£175 and as such I would pay you about £75–£85 for it.'

That would have given me a profit of £40 at least on the purchase price.

A PC 49 soap which cost me £7 at a boot sale was also appreciated by Lisa Silver, who explained, 'It's in excellent condition and the policeman is always popular. This I know I could sell quickly and would expect to charge a customer £15–£18, but that would mean me paying just £7–£8.' So, the Ladybird house offered a profit, but the PC 49 soap would simply be a case of getting back the money I had paid originally.

A Snow White toothbrush holder dating from the 1930s, which had been bought three years previously for £90, was offered to Arthur Selby, a specialist at the time in Disneyana. He explained, 'I bought one of those this morning funnily enough and would expect a Snow White to go for between £100 and £125, but I'd pay only £75–£90. The market has changed a lot. eBay and the other Internet auctions have opened up the whole market. It means that prices have flattened a lot in the middle range and many items once thought of as rare are now not so uncommon. At one time, any of the 1930s Disney toothbrush holders could make £150+ and some, such as Snow White, were selling for nearer £300, but the Internet has seen that prices have come right back down again.'

What had become abundantly clear from the 5 a.m. start on an extremely wet, cold and windy day in Newark was that having an end buyer is the key to securing a lucrative deal for both the collector and the dealer. Knowing just what buyers a dealer might have lined up who are looking for items for a collection is another matter. As Arthur Selby says, 'I always ask people what they want for an item rather than simply offer a price. Firstly, I'm not here to simply value people's collections for them and secondly what I know is hard-earned information. The only thing a dealer really has is his knowledge and it's from that, and the mistakes we've made along the way, that we make our living. We can't be expected to act as a general reference guide and I always find that those collectors who really want to sell already know what they want for an item anyway.'

Top tip: Overall, I felt I had not done too badly. I'd got my money back on the PC 49 soap and the Snow White toothbrush holder. Furthermore, I'd made £40 on the Ladybird house. However, simply getting into the Newark Antiques Fair on the Monday, the day reserved for dealers and not the general public, cost £20. Then there was the petrol money from London and the overnight hotel stay of £42. Suddenly, it became obvious why so many dealers, including Lisa Silver, stay in their cars overnight on the Newark site. It can be the difference between breaking even and making money. Certainly, as a collector trying to sell pieces for a profit, I'd learnt that this was far from an easy way to make money. Furthermore, I came away with the lasting impression that any profit the dealers make is hard earned and well deserved – particularly when the night-time temperatures reach minus five. DMG Antiques Fairs Ltd holds trade fairs which take place mid-week throughout the year and are often the focus of *Bargain Hunt's* filming across the country. For a list of future fair dates around the country, stand and ticket information, contact DMG at PO Box 100, Newark, Nottinghamshire NG24 1DJ. Tel: 01636 702326 or www.dmgantiquefairs.com.

SELLING TO A SPECIALIST DEALER

Searching the Internet will again help you make contact with specialist dealers, the vast majority of whom run their own websites and will explain how they work and how to make an appointment to get a valuation. Many may request a photo to be sent first. Alternatively, collectables guidebooks such as

Miller's Collectables Price Guide, published annually, has a list of specialist dealers at the back and the *Antiques Trade Gazette* website can also offer up such contacts. In theory, specialists are highly regarded within the trade simply because they are usually the leading experts in their chosen field and as such know more than anyone else about that particular era, area or topic. By default they are usually in contact with the world's largest collectors within their specialist field and are therefore the ones most able to offer the top price for an item, knowing that they can then sell it on to a collector quickly and efficiently.

Top tip: Do beware, as not all dealers, whether generalists or specialists, are honest. Exercise caution and in the worst-case scenario get legal advice. In 2002 Kim-John Webb was convicted of deception for ascribing scrap value to a watch which was worth £20,000 thanks to its connection with the *Titanic.* The lady who had inherited the watch but was unaware of its value had taken it to Webb to have it valued. The silver Benson watch was originally presented from the Countess of Rothes to a crew member, Alfred Crawford, for manning the *Titanic* lifeboat in which the Countess was rescued. Webb recognised the watch's calibre but valued it at the silver scrap value of £15. However, early in the year Henry Aldridge & Son Auctioneers had sold an almost identical watch given by the Countess to another seaman in the lifeboat, Thomas Jones, for £22,000. Andrew Aldridge, of Henry Aldridge & Son Auctioneers, explains, 'It was the fact that we had sold the Jones watch for that sort of figure that saw the jury uphold the prosecution's argument that the dealer had full knowledge of the watch's significance and had actively deceived the seller.' In 1999 the defaced watch failed to find a buyer. It seems that despite its historic *Titanic* connection, Webb had taken such care to remove the all-important engraving marking the provenance of the watch that few collectors were prepared to bid on the item.

SELLING TO COLLECTOR-DEALERS

The best prices are usually paid by collectors. There's a logic to this. A piece submitted at auction may be purchased by a dealer, who then takes it to a fair and sells it to a member of the public/collector. If the piece cost £100 at auction then the auction house has charged the dealer 10% so the cost to the dealer is £110. The dealer has to fund and cover the cost of his travelling to the antiques fair and his pitch, which may be anything from £40 to £500 for a large fair such as those held at the NEC in Birmingham. Therefore, a further percentage will be added to the piece. It may have cost £100 hammer price but by now it's probably marked at £140–£200 in order for the dealer to cover his costs to date and make a profit.

Some dealers work on the basis of 'turnover'. Whatever they buy they will simply add 10–30% on every single piece, regardless of the original purchase price, so that their stock turns over quickly. Others are happy to double the purchase price and sit on the stock until it sells, which may be within a month or take several years.

It means that collectors are generally those who pay the top prices or full retail price for a collectable. This reflects the fact that a lot of groundwork has gone into finding the item, perhaps restoring it or cleaning it, and then presenting it at a venue for collectors where it can be bought and enjoyed instantly.

Those wishing to sell an item should try and aim at selling it direct to another collector for the best price and the lowest fees. Joining clubs is a great way of meeting and contacting the collectors most likely to be seeking the items you have. Royal Doulton and Moorcroft, for example, each have a collectors' club which sees its members not only getting special offers and limited editions but also a newsletter that allows them to contact other collectors who are seeking items, selling or buying. Clearly, an element of trust is involved but it's a system that works well and enables people to know that their piece is going to be appreciated by a collector and that they have probably got within the upper price range for the item.

Top tip: Vic Jelenski, keen boot-saler and eBay enthusiast, explains, 'I purchased a fantastic item from a boot sale. It was a piece of Border Fine Arts and as I was also a member of the Border Fine Arts Club I had the quarterly newsletter to hand. The exact piece I had bought for £5 was being sought by another collector in the "Wanted" section of the club magazine, so I made contact and sold the piece the next day to him for £1,000. It was such a great profit and such a quick turnaround and made complete sense compared to listing the item on the Internet – very often it's all about making and building contacts, finding the right seller and being happy to take a profit quickly, rather than being greedy and spending a lot of time phoning round, listing items on the Internet in the mean hope of getting an extra fiver.'

At the end of the day, if the collection is no longer wanted or the item was inherited, whatever money is made is extra money that you didn't have, whether or not you get the very best price for the pieces.

Don't be greedy. Buying is a pleasure but selling means you're getting involved in the business side of the antiques and collecting world where time is money and everyone needs to make a living.

Conclusion

- eBay's 'completed items' section is one of the best places to start checking out the potential value of your items – if you don't have a computer, local libraries and Internet cafes are a good place to start.
- Collectors' guidebooks are invaluable but expensive, so order them from your local library. This may take time but is a better idea than investing hundreds of pounds in books you may need only once to check a particular item.
- Remember that most auction houses will value items, for non-insurance purposes, free of charge so make the most of this service.
- Allow plenty of time for items to be valued properly – time is money, but getting it wrong could cost you thousands.

- Check your household insurance policy to ensure that you are sufficiently covered for the items you have, should you discover they are worth more than you thought.

CHAPTER SIX
SELLING ON EBAY

Part One: Hosting your Auction – Listing your eBay Items

If you believe everything you read in the newspapers, selling on eBay is the new Holy Grail. It brings fortunes to sellers and has no downside. Of course the truth is somewhat different. Yes, it's true that eBay has given many people a whole new form of income, either part-time or full-time, and that it's possible to turn over thousands of pounds a month, but as with most Holy Grails there is a catch.

Vic Jelenski has been selling on eBay for the last five years and explains:

It's an amazing tool, but you have to move with the market changes. I started off selling a lot of my own personal collections – ceramic items, Royal Doulton figures, Border Fine Arts that sort of thing – but nowadays I'm getting a better profit margin from children's toys such as Lego, which I am selling by the pound to places as far flung as Australia. It's easy for people to think it's easy money, but to make a full-time living you need to be visiting and buying from hundreds of boot sales during the summer and working flat out to list your stuff and then pack and post it during the winter months and all that takes time. Personally, I love it and can't think of anything I'd rather do, but if you're not into boot sales and collecting, it could become as humdrum as any other job.

There's no doubt that eBay, which is only ten years old, has become the largest medium available to traders for buying and selling. The site has 125 million people registered, although this number is growing daily, and boasts worldwide trade in more than 50,000 categories. In the USA there are 430,000 users and thousands more around the globe are making either all or most of their income on the site. Its legendary beginnings came in 1995 when Pierre Omidyar tried to track down contacts for his wife, who was an avid Pez collector. She wanted to interact with other collectors over the Internet and so the idea of eBay was born. The very first item to sell was Pierre's broken laser pointer which made $14. Since then, millions of items have been sold, including a plastic Tesco supermarket bag which made £4.39. The bag was sold by thirty-year-old Jamie Green and bidding started at 1p. Then there was the bottle full of water that had been taken from the Diana Memorial Fountain in London. It realised £248 on eBay. Then there was the £15,000 paid to Diana Duyser of Hollywood, Florida, by an

Internet casino company for a ten-year-old cheese toastie said to bear the image of Jesus's mother Mary. The starting price was £2,000 and the auction received 1.7 million hits before closing. The fact that the piece of toast went to a company is reminiscent of the Internet company that paid £13,000 for David Beckham's boots from the 1999 season in which Manchester United won the treble. This headline figure ensured plenty of publicity for the Internet company, which then offered the boots up as a prize. Three years later the lucky winner submitted the boots back to Christie's for auction, where they realised £1,500. The point here is that just because something is sold for a certain price does not mean that it is worth this amount. If you are going to be a successful eBayer, you need to bear in mind that some sales are gimmicks while others indicate there really is a market for a particular type of product.

Let's be honest – if everyone could raid Tescos for its free bags and sell every one for £4.39, there would be no need to work! Clearly, these items, while amusing, are only going to hit the headlines or get such staggering results once. Don't give up the day job in the hope of living off Tesco bags. eBay is monitored closely and responsibly but there will always be weird and wacky items appearing for sale – and not all of it in good taste. Attempts to sell a kidney, a child and a girl's virginity on eBay have all been banned. eBay itself has a long list of items that cannot be sold on its site, including firearms, but where there's a will there's a way and it can take the ebay.com organisation a while to realise just how people are working a way around the rules. For example, in the early days of eBay people listed gun cases for sale – which was perfectly legitimate. However, it gradually became clear that many of these gun cases were realising disproportionate amounts thanks to the fact that certain sellers were including 'free' guns with the case!

Clearly, responsible individuals will shun selling items that are stolen, fake, counterfeit, or simply likely to offend others and although the Internet is a worldwide medium it's still possible for people to be prosecuted for crimes that take place in their own country. For example, if someone in the UK were to knowingly sell stolen items on eBay, they could still be charged with handling stolen goods. Sometimes, it's just a case of having some common sense about what you are selling. Unfortunately, this was lacking in the case of one royal aide who sold his Fortnum & Mason Christmas pudding on eBay only to find it had cost him his job! It seems that every year Her Majesty distributes the £6.25 puddings to her 1,450 staff accompanied by a note that reads 'Best Wishes for Christmas and the New Year from The Queen and Duke of Edinburgh'. A spokesman for Buckingham Palace explained, 'Disciplinary action was taken following an incident where a Christmas pudding was placed on eBay.'

Such is the eBay fever at present that even the British Museum was forced last October to issue a general plea to people to stop selling ancient artefacts on eBay. Last year, some 47,000 ancient artefacts were dug up by amateur archaeologists and metal detectorists. Most of these were recovered responsibly with permission having been requested and granted by the landowners and the finds were then submitted under the Treasure Act. Nevertheless, as with any hobby or profession, there are always a few bad apples. The British Museum had good reason to suspect that many of the items listed on eBay, including a Viking bronze horse-harness pendant and a fourteenth-century hollow-shank bronze door key, had been recovered by detectorists and not reported under the

Treasure Act of 1996. This act requires finders to report potential treasure finds that are more than 300 years old. Unfortunately, despite its pleas, the British Museum was told by eBay that only if the items can be proved to fall within the criteria of the Treasure Act can it remove the listed items. Clearly, this would involve more time and resources than either the British Museum or eBay can spare. What eBay does say is, 'Whenever we are informed by any authoritative third party that they believe an item to be illegal, we take that item down.' However, proving the illegality of an item can be a long and drawn-out process.

Despite all of this, there are still plenty of opportunities for people to, quite simply, turn their old clutter into cash through the eBay site. In the early days, of course, there were plenty of imitators keen to get on the eBay bandwagon, including the likes of auctionworld.com and qxl.com, but none were able to come near eBay's success. It's hard to see how any company will ever be able to rival eBay unless a keener, younger company can undercut the Internet site while providing access to millions of potential bidders at the same time. To a great extent eBay's success has been to recognise its own weaknesses and address them swiftly.

There's no doubt that selling on eBay is something just about everyone wants to have a go at, whether or not they turn it into a full-time job. I work with eBay enthusiast and cameraman Craig Harman, who has also worked on the TV show *Most Haunted*. He says, 'Everyone is always going on about ebay.com and I had a *Most Haunted* crew jacket that I certainly didn't want to wear, so I thought I'd have a go and put it on eBay, where to my surprise it got a bid of £120 immediately and then sold for £350. It's easy to see how people get hooked because I would not have thought it possible to sell something I got for nothing for such a substantial amount.' Not every sale is a joy, however, and you have to feel sorry for John Pearson who sold a BMW once owned by David Beckham for £16,000 only to see it realise £90,000 on eBay a few weeks later. Pearson was not a stupid fellow – he'd done his research and had approached several BMW dealers to get an idea of its value, only to be told that the car, despite the provenance, was worth only around £12,000.

You can buy and sell absolutely anything within reason through eBay. A mobile phone sells every minute, a CD every 11 seconds and a piece of golf equipment every 2.5 minutes. The top-selling unusual items are a Gulf Jet Stream, which made an incredible $4.9m, David Beckham's football as used in the penalty shoot-out (the football that missed) in Euro 2004, which sold for £18,700 and Lady Thatcher's handbag, which fetched £103,000. *GMTV*'s presenter Penny Smith offered a date with herself and some lucky person won the night out for a mere £9,000. Not quite the same amount as was once bid for a photograph of myself snapped at a boot sale. Nevertheless, even that sold – so perhaps it really is a case of anything can sell on eBay!

Before you attempt to sell something on eBay, give yourself a day to get a good idea of the market you are about to enter:

Get onto a computer with Internet access. If you haven't one yourself, go to an Internet café or check out whether your local library has Internet access.

Click on the Internet access icon on the main screen, which should bring up the Internet provider, for example AOL or Wanadoo among others.

Go to the address bar, which is usually a strip located in the middle of the top, and type in www.ebay.com.

Either using the site map or by going into your search engine again take the time to also check out www.ebay.co.uk as this is the part of the ebay.com site that is specific to the UK alone. Here you will find sellers who are in theory only listing the items they are selling within the geographical confines of the UK itself.

Compare the prices of past sales under 'completed items' for similar items listed under www.ebay.com and www.ebay.co.uk as sometimes there can be a difference in the auction result. The ebay.com market clearly attracts bidders from around the world whereas www.ebay.co.uk is restricted to bidding and buying within the UK only – making a comparison will help you decide whether you want to list under the worldwide market or just the UK.

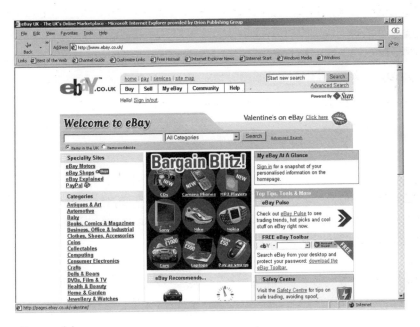

eBay.co.uk home page.

On www.ebay.com you have access to the main worldwide eBay site, which will cover every single item listed for auction from around the world. All sorts of options are open to you in terms of checking out categories, listings, shops, etc but I personally prefer to simply go on the eBay 'search' box and type in the item I am looking for or trying to research. I should warn you that browsing through ebay.com can see you getting through more hours of the day and night than you would have thought possible. To start with, having a good old browse around is to be recommended but in the long term you will find that time management is essential if you are going to make the most of selling on eBay. That means restricting yourself to the jobs listed below rather than getting distracted by the amazing and interesting things going on within the site itself.

FIRST THINGS FIRST

You really do need to own a computer with the Internet installed to get yourself started for selling on eBay. The price of computers and going online has, of course, come down tremendously in recent years.

It's possible to get interest-free credit on many deals with computer companies and stores, which is a great way to get started. It means small monthly payments with no interest charged. Do check the small print, though, as if you fail to pay the entire amount off within the interest-free period interest charges may then kick in, which makes it very costly.

It's also preferable to buy a new computer and start from scratch rather than taking a chance with a second-hand computer from a source that you do not know.

Once this is up and running you will be ready to start the registration process to become a seller on eBay. You cannot register with eBay until you have a working email address. These are simple to set up and many Internet sites offer free email services.

Find a site such as Yahoo or Hotmail that supply this free service and follow the easy instructions to obtain your email address. Make sure that you keep a note of your address and the password otherwise you will have to re-register another one. This email address is also particularly important, as it is where all the 'questions for sellers' come through to; you need to open up on a daily basis.

Once you have obtained your email address you are ready to open up www.ebay.co.uk and register.

Registering on eBay

You are confronted with a home page and at the very top is the word 'register'. Click on this and it will take you into a form that needs to be completed in order to start the registration process.

This form allows you only to bid and not actually to sell. When you get to the 'selling form' you need a debit or credit card to enter onto the file before you can start selling your items and making money.

The 'registration form' is very straightforward and simply requires personal details such as name, address and your new email details.

Once you have filled this in you will then be asked to read and agree the 'user agreement'.

Once this is completed you then click the relevant boxes to prove that you have done so and click 'continue'. This is the first step to completing an eBay account.

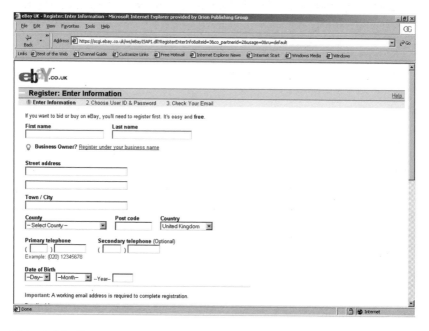

eBay registration page.

eBay user name

This is possibly the most time-consuming part of the registration process. Each person registered has to have a different ID name so that no two sellers are alike or have the same user information. eBay itself provides you with some options that you can choose or if you prefer you can think up one of your own. This can prove difficult, as with 125 million registered users you have to find an ID name that no one else has thought of already and that is not deemed obscene, so choose carefully.

Top tip: Try to choose something that is personal to you for your eBay user name and not something that anyone would be able to guess immediately as being connected to you. Personally, I keep a separate note of my eBay user name tucked away in a safe place just in case I forget it, which is easy to do if you have a break from selling on the site.

eBay password

Try not to use the same password as on your email address. In this way, if someone gains access (this rarely happens unless you answer a fake email) then they cannot gain access into both your eBay account and your email.

You will then be asked to enter a 'secret question' and 'secret answer'. This again is to ensure that the site remains secure and only you will know the answers.

Once you have completed these steps then you click 'continue', which takes you onto the final page.

A confirmation email is sent to your email address. This has a registration code.

Click onto 'complete eBay registration'. This confirms with eBay that your email is valid and you then become a fully fledged member of the eBay community.

Top tip: For the first few sales you make on eBay try and keep everything really simple and opt for the most basic options until your confidence grows. The most important goal initially is to make that first sale and ensure that you get the money you want and that the buyer is happy with the purchase.

Selling on eBay

Even though you are now registered you are not classed as a seller. There is another process that has to be completed before you can start loading on all those items for selling.

At the top of the home page there is the word 'sell'. Click onto this and it takes you straight into another form – the 'selling form'.

It asks you how you would like to sell your item – 'auction' or 'fixed price'. You choose the option you prefer, normally 'auction' and click 'sell your item'.

This takes you to 'create a seller's account'. Click this and then eBay will ask for your user ID and password where indicated. Once you have entered this information click 'sign in securely'.

This then takes you into a further from, which asks for credit or debit card details. This system is very secure so no one will be able to access it and use your card. You simply fill out the details and press 'continue'. Now you are ready to sell.

Top tip: There are various selling help categories in the 'site map', so any questions that you may have can usually be answered through this system. Also, some people run eBay conferences to help beginners get started but you should be able to sell on your own without attending such seminars as it is pretty self-explanatory. Go to ebay.co.uk > Home > Help > eBay Explained > How Do I Sell?

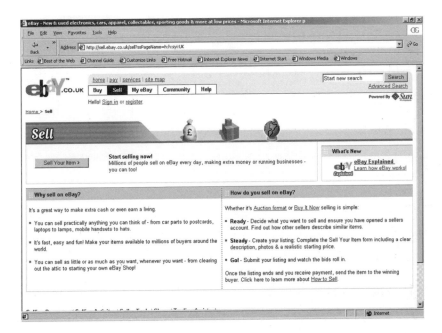

eBay selling page.

Type of Auction

There are several different types of auction, which include a straightforward or fixed-price auction. All are really simple to use and it just takes a bit of time to decide which one will work best for you.

A straightforward auction is what most people tend to use. When loading on your items you simply click this box and it then gives you an option of how many days you would like the auction to run for. You can choose between one, three, five, seven or ten days. Look at when the auction will finish and work out whether it has a good finishing time or not.

A fixed-price auction is when there is no normal auction format with bidding, just a 'Buy It Now' option. This allows the seller to set the price that they want for an item in the hope that it will sell quickly and they will not have to wait for an auction to finish. Buyers can then just purchase the item outright. Sellers can also sell multiple items using this process and the 'Buy It Now' icon does not disappear when one item from a multiple listing has been purchased. A seller has to have a minimum feedback rating of ten or have placed direct-debit details on file to use this fixed-price format.

> *Top tip:* Tracy Martin sells regularly on eBay and recommends that an auction should finish on a Sunday evening, as most people are at home and not working. If you start the auction on a Thursday evening and place it on for ten days this will ensure that it finishes on a Sunday; it also incorporates two weekends, which gives buyers a chance to see the item. Place it on in the evening at around 9 p.m. or 10 p.m. as this also gives the USA bidders a chance.

Photographs

Pictures are a large part of the selling process on eBay. Buyers like to see what they are spending their money on, so good, clear pictures are essential.

Invest in a high-quality digital camera which takes close-up macro shots and that can be connected to your computer.

These usually come with their own software, which is simply loaded on by disc and then once you have mastered the camera you can click away. The camera can then be connected to the computer either through a lead or an additional drive (this depends on the camera and software). You can transfer your pictures to the computer and save them or put them directly on to eBay from the camera itself if it has an additional drive.

When taking the pictures, make sure that you have good lighting and clear shots as this answers many questions for sellers and they can see exactly what the item is. The old saying 'a picture tells a thousand words' is certainly true when trading on eBay.

If the item has any damage, take a separate photograph so that you can point out the problem. If china, take a picture of the base with the markings confirming that it is an authentic piece. If selling clothes, take close-up pictures of the outfit as well as a shot of the whole item of clothing. You can also take pictures of the labels, especially if the item is a designer outfit.

Top tip: The more the buyer can see, the higher the chance of your item selling for a good price so ensure that you take pictures of everything that you feel is relevant for securing a good sale. Remember to include the measurements of the item too, as a photograph cannot give the potential buyer any indication of the piece's actual size. By including these details in your description you can avoid a lot of individual emails from potential buyers.

The first of these photos shows how best to display the item you are selling. To avoid the mistakes made in the other two photographs, do not use blurred pictures and make sure that it is clear which item is for sale.

Photograph fees

For the first picture that you place along with your listing there is no cost. This is offered free from eBay but additional pictures will cost you 12p.

The 'gallery' option is also used quite frequently by sellers. It allows buyers to see your item photograph next to a listing in the results page, alerting them to what is for sale without having to click into the auction page to find out. This service costs 15p.

There is an additional gallery service. This is 'gallery featured' at a cost of £15.95. This service ensures that your item appears in the special featured section above the gallery; it is double the size and also appears in the general gallery below.

If this is too expensive, you could use the option for 'supersize image' at 60p each, which shows buyers full-sized, detailed pictures. This display size is up to 4 x 3 inches (10 x 8 cm).

You can decide that you wish to use a 'picture show'. This is when you have taken a few pictures of the item at different angles and the buyer can view these as a slide show, seeing every angle of your item as it turns. This will cost you 15p for each picture and you have to use more than two to take full advantage of this service.

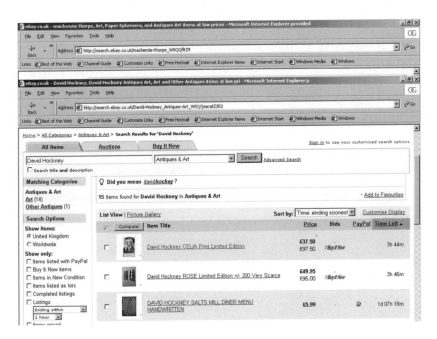 The final option is 'picture pack', which offers you the maximum exposure of the item selling and includes the supersize images, along with picture show and gallery. You can add up to twelve images to this and it costs 90p for up to six images and £1.35 for seven to twelve images.

Gallery – search results page featuring gallery-listed photographs.

Top tip: If the above costs are a little expensive then use the free picture with eBay and offer to email additional pictures to any interested bidders.

PREPARATION

You now want to sell something and the best thing to do is try and do some research before listing the item. You can easily check similar items that have sold by clicking into the 'completed items'; this shows prices that items have ended on previously and gives you an idea of what the item is worth.

You can also research your piece by looking at others who have sold the same thing and get any information that you are unsure of, especially what the best price is for that particular piece. This information obtained from other sellers can help with why one item exactly the same as another might sell for less. For example, a lot of people make spelling mistakes in their titles so a buyer looking might not come across what they want purely because of misspelt listings.

> *Top tip:* Do not cut and paste the details or photographs of other completed auctions listed by other sellers and use these yourself unless you have the seller's permission. eBay can and will remove your listing if you have clearly copied verbatim the details and photographs of another seller.

Auction category

The auction categories are a great help too, so, if you are selling a car, don't just list it generally – make the most of the eBay Motors UK site to list your car. This is now the most visited UK retail website for cars and therefore has a vast traffic of potential buyers looking to purchase vehicles. Paul Hayes, the antiques expert on *Cash in the Attic,* has this tip:

I sold my red Mercedes classic 200 TE Estate car from 1983 on eBay, emphasising of course that the buyer had to collect. It sold for £315, which is more than I was offered for it scrap, and the buyer came to my house with a low loader and took it away. It cost only about £15 in eBay charges to sell it and that too was a lot less than it would have cost me to advertise it in the local paper or the classic-car magazines. I was so impressed I then bought my latest car for £2,500 on ebay.com. Although I did have to go from Lancashire to Surrey to collect it, I saved £1,000 on the price it would have cost me to buy the same model from a car showroom. What is important for people to remember, though, is to read the small print very carefully when buying larger goods as I once nearly bid on a scooter only to find that the buyer had to collect it from Ohio!

Once you have taken your photos and you have all the information that you need for your item, you are ready to load your listing onto eBay.

Press 'sell your item' and then decide which auction type you wish to use. Choose a category – the range is vast and includes Collectables, Pottery and Porcelain to Weird Stuff and Music.

Choose the category carefully and check that the item you are going to be selling will complement or is similar to other items listed in this category.

If your item fits into two categories then you can add a second for an additional fee.

Top tip: Many UK buyers and sellers prefer to restrict their activities to the UK alone and therefore list only on ebay.co.uk. This is partly because the time involved processing money and for postal delivery is overall a lot quicker internally within this country. It can take up to three weeks for money and items to arrive to or from America and that's by plane – by sea transportation it can be up to three months in some cases.

Auction item title

Once you have found and completed the category section you must fill in the 'item descriptive title' – this is very important as it is usually what buyers use to search.

Make sure that you write what your item is; include manufacturer's name and any key words that will entice the buyer to look at your particular auction.

There is also the option to put in a second subtitle; this costs an extra 50p. It does not, however, show up when buyers type in a search for a specific item but simply shows in small letters under your title. It is really additional information for the buyer.

Top tip: Capital letters make your listing stand out from the others and is free. Don't exaggerate or enhance descriptions, as this can mean successful bidders may then question the truth of your description. For example, if something is an antique is needs to be 100 years old and a 1950s Bossons wall plaque is not 'Art Deco'.

Auction description

Underneath your header title you will see a box for adding the description of your item. This again is extremely important and you need to be accurate about the item that you are selling. Put as much information in as possible: what the item is, how old it is, is there any damage and any other things that you feel might help to sell it.

Try to get as much information into your title as possible: use every key word that you can think of to encourage buyers to look.

Do not withhold information, as the buyer will simply want a refund or problems will arise in the future. The key is to be as honest as you can. The description can make a huge difference to an item.

It is important to get the information correct when typing the description. If there is any damage, such as hairline cracks to china or tears to clothing, you must point this out and put another picture into the listing showing the damage. If you make people aware of any such problems there can be no comeback from the buyer that the piece is not perfect.

Measure the size of the item, write about any relevant information that you feel would encourage the buyer to bid on your item and ensure that the dates and markings are included.

If you are unsure of a piece then let the buyer know that you think the description is correct but would welcome any further information from others. Normally in this case buyers will email you to let you know if something in the description is wrong so that you can update the item description.

Always include information on what payment methods you will accept. If you have no means of taking or processing credit-card payments, make this clear. Similarly, if you wish to accept only cheques or postal orders, explain this.

Include details of minimum anticipated postage and packaging charges or on larger pieces make it clear whether the buyer must collect or whether transport can be arranged but at further cost.

Make your descriptions friendly but not too gushing or overly personal – professional descriptions are best.

Many people argue that reading any length of text in bold, underlined or capital fonts can be difficult, so make sure your description layout is clear, concise, informative and not splattered with coloured text or lots of moving images.

Remember that some items are prohibited on eBay, such as livestock, etc.

Some items that are not necessarily banned by eBay are nevertheless illegal for sale in this country, including ivory unless it is antique.

Some items, including certain taxidermy pieces, may require specialist export permission if being sold outside the UK.

Knowingly selling items that are fakes, forgeries, counterfeit or stolen is just as much a criminal offence on eBay as it is at any other sale forum.

Top tip: Recently there was a case where a buyer took a seller to court because they accused the seller of mis-description. The item for sale was described as 'a mint X-box' but when the buyer received the item believing it to be the X-Box console he found only an empty box that would have housed the console. The case was won by the seller as he had described it properly as a mint X-Box and there was no mention of the console coming with the empty box.

Listing fees

Start the auction off low or with no reserve – a reserve is when you set a price below which the item cannot sell.

Alternatively, start the auction with the minimum price that you wish to secure in order to part with the item. For example, if you have an expensive piece of china and you do not want to sell it for less than £50, you can place a reserve of £50 but start the bidding low at £4.99. Only once it has been bid up to the £50 will that item sell. If the reserve price is not met then you do not have to part with the item to a buyer.

There is an additional fee for reserve auctions, which is added on to the listing fee but if the item does sell then your reserve fee is credited back to your account. You now cannot add a reserve unless the reserve price is £50 or over. For an item with a reserve between £50 and £4,999.99 then the cost is 2% of the reserve price. If it is £5,000 or over then the set reserve price fee is £100.

With any item that you list for sale fees are payable. These are calculated by the minimum bid that you start your auction at.

Prices start at 15p per listing for an item starting at between 1p and 99p, then the payment structure goes up as follows:

£1.00–£4.99	20p
£5.00–£14.99	35p
£15.00–£29.99	75p
£30.00–£99.99	£1.50
£100+	£2.00

These are simply listing fees – additional features such as gallery, reserve and 'Buy It Now' all cost extra.

A separate charge is made on the final auction price. The fee structure is in percentage costs and is the following:

£0.01–£29.99	5.25% of the final auction price
£30.00–£599.99	5.25% for the first £29.99 (£1.57) plus 3.25% of the remaining closing balance.
£600+	5.25% for the first £29.99 (£1.57) plus 3.25% of the initial £30.00 to £599.99 (£18.53) plus 1.75% of the remaining closing balance.

If your item fails to sell then you have the opportunity to list it again free of eBay charges.

If your buyer fails to complete the deal then you can reclaim any charges paid to eBay providing you can supply the necessary proof that the sale has fallen through and that this is not your fault.

Sometimes eBay offers sellers a 'Free Listing Day' which means no fees are charged when you place the item up for sale, although you will still have to pay fees for additional features and an end-of-auction fee.

Should you be interested in trying it out for yourself eBay will advertise the day in advance on its home page and send you an email telling you exactly when this day is happening and when it starts and finishes.

Top tip: **eBay enthusiast Vic Jelenski, who now buys and sells on ebay.co.uk full-time, suggests, 'I only use the free listing days to sell the items that I consider to be pretty low-end in terms of value. I use these days to get rid of stuff that has been hanging around or that I have not sold. There are so many people selling on free listing days that it's a really competitive market and there's really an oversupply of items coming up for sale so the prices paid are generally lower. But it's certainly a great way of clearly unsold stuff.'**

Personally, my first eBay sale was a Royal Winton wall clock bought at Portobello Road antiques market for £80. I listed the piece on ebay.com as most of the top Royal Winton collectors tend to be American. Having uploaded the picture and description I sat back and waited and one week later the clock had been bought by an American buyer for £188. Taking into account the eBay charges at the time, which came to £2.98, and the fact that the buyer had to pay the postage and packing costs I made a clear profit of £105. My second sale was a Wadeheath

Disney Snow White butter dish bought at auction for £220. It took me a day to list the item properly, as I researched the history of Wadeheath, and the backstamp details and took plenty of good photographs to include in the description. A week later it had sold to an Italian for £390. The fees which were paid to eBay worked out at £7.29 and were deducted automatically from my credit card, leaving a profit of £162.71.

Part 2: Going, Going, Gone! – Completing Your Auction

DURING THE AUCTION

It's likely that you will get emails from potential bidders who wish to know more information, details or estimates for the postage and packaging. It can be a frustrating task, as you may well have given all the details and the costs of postage in your description already. It's tempting to email such bidders back curtly requesting that they read your description properly. However, remember that this email is from a potential bidder – a person who might make all the difference to the end result of your auction.

If you are going to be away, busy or unable to access your email during the auction listing it's worth noting this on the description so that potential bidders don't think you are simply ignoring them. A simple line will do: 'I will be unable to answer any questions or emails relating to this auction until…'

Top tip: Collectables specialist Martin Donovan says, 'I am often asked by UK buyers whether they can come and pick the item up directly rather than wait for me to send the item. I assess each individual case. Sometimes a bidder may be desperate to get the item because it is for a birthday or anniversary so I will arrange to meet somewhere within my home county but never actually give out my full address or allow any bidder to visit my home. This to me is just common sense because at the end of the day, no matter how many items they have bought from me I don't really know that person. Mind you, just before Christmas I met a gentleman and his wife on the M25 to hand over a 'Wol Signs The Rissolution' that they had bought for £110. They had travelled all the way from Worcestershire to Essex just to pick it up and when I asked them why, they said that they simply didn't trust the postal service to deliver it safely as in the past items sent registered post have mysteriously disappeared.'

Get to know your bidders – it's great watching the price of the item you have listed rise in value as more and more people bid and it's worth opting to have a counter option on your listing. The counter option can be picked up when you are listing your item for sale and it will then allow you to see just how many people have taken a look at your item and also lets others know that there is a lot of interest.

Check the feedback on anyone who has made a bid for your item. Those with little feedback may well be new to eBay and you should bear this in mind, but if you have bidders who have had a lot of negative feedback you can block them from bidding.

You need to be careful and have good reasons for blocking a bidder as you want to ensure the maximum exposure for your auction. However, some eBayers do not have particularly good feedback, or you may find that they do not proceed with the sale and let you down. Go to Help > Selling > Managing Your Listing > Managing Bidders > Block Bidders.

It's not good form to withdraw an item once it is listed but there may be justifiable reasons for doing this. You may have found damage that you had not previously noticed or, as can happen, the piece is accidentally damaged beyond repair. Under such circumstances eBay can help and details of how to proceed can be found on its help and advice pages. However, this needs to be done at least twelve hours before the item auction ends. Go to Help > Selling > Managing Your Item > Ending Your Listing Early.

Top tip: Never be tempted to 'bid up' your own item or to enlist other eBayers to bid for your item when they are not genuinely interested in buying it. You have every right to bring your auction to the attention of people who you think may be interested in what you have to sell. However, if you then directly or indirectly (for example, using another identity or eBay user name) bid on your own item – or bid on an item for someone else attempting to 'bid up' their own listing, you can be banned. You are falsely bidding to increase the price and eBay can ban you from using its site for doing this.

UNSOLD

If your item doesn't sell, you need to consider why this may be. Despite all the headlines, not everything will sell on eBay. You can always list the item again but bear in mind you may need to make amendments and learn from the experience. Even American actor Christian Slater has had this problem. He listed his *Star Wars* toy collection on eBay and none of it sold. So ask yourself:

 Was the reserve too high? Check other comparable pieces on 'completed items' to see if this might be the case.

 Were the pictures poor or the description lacking in detail?

 Did I use the wrong category or misspell the title description, making it impossible to pick up under a general search of the site for similar items?

 Did my auction end at a bad time for potential UK bidders?

 Is it the wrong time of year to be selling? Many eBayers argue that August is a dead month for selling as so many people take their annual holidays at this point and are not online.

 Did I allow enough time? Bear in mind that pre-Christmas most people will give up bidding on items that they are buying for Christmas presents by the first week in December as postal delivery in time for Christmas can rarely be guaranteed.

SOLD

 Once the auction has finished and your item has been sold

you receive an email from eBay with details of the winning bidder.

Contact the winning bidder via the email system, providing them with postage costs and your address if it is not already explained in your listing page.

The winning bidder will advise you of the payment method that they will be using subject to any restrictions you may have put on payment methods in your description.

When the money has cleared through your account you can then send the item out to them and hopefully complete a successful transaction. Good feedback may then be left about seller and buyer.

Top tip: Never send out items until the money has cleared in your bank account. Most UK eBayers are patient enough to understand emails outlining this and will expect you to clear the money first. However, many American buyers and worldwide buyers paying through PayPal can get very impatient if you ask them to wait until the money has cleared in your account: they consider that the minute the money is delivered into the PayPal account the item is paid for. This is one of the reasons why many UK eBayers prefer to buy and sell within the UK alone.

TRANSFERRING AND RECEIVING MONEY

Money can be transferred and sent in many forms today, including:

Business cheques. Many people who buy and sell on eBay for a living have business accounts and therefore use business cheques. Rarely do business cheques have any form of guarantee, so you will need to ensure that these are banked and cleared before sending an item.

Personal cheques. Items under £100 can be guaranteed with a cheque card and even if the buyer has written the guarantee number on the back you personally have not seen the card so again you should wait for this to clear first.

Postal orders. These come in denominations ranging from 50p to £20 and you as the person cashing in the postal order will get the full face value indicated on the order. However, bear in mind that should you need to reimburse a buyer this way there are fees payable for buying a postal order which range from 25p for the lowest denomination to £1.25 for a £20 postal order.

Money orders. These are costly to buy and costly to bank for eBay sellers. The charges UK banks levy to accept a money order into your personal account can vary. The advantage is that a money order from a British bank is as good as cash but the disadvantage is that it will cost you to bank it, and therefore eat into your profit. In the case of international money orders it becomes prohibitive for most eBayers. In addition, accepting money orders from abroad can mean lengthy waits to receive the order by post and delay the whole process of completing the sale.

Electronic transfer. This is not to be recommended because it necessitates the person wishing to send the money having information on your personal bank account and potentially this lays you open to fraud.

Cash in the post. Don't go there, as there is no guarantee that the money will arrive. However, some people still do send cash in the post so remember that the onus is on the winning bidder to get the money to you and should the cash go 'missing' it's down to the winning bidder not you to ensure the completion of the deal.

PayPal. This is a money-transfer system. Both buyers and sellers set up an account and this allows buyers to pay for their auction wins and allows sellers to receive money from UK and abroad. This system is widely acclaimed for being totally secure and offering eBay sellers a means of accepting debit and credit cards. There is a small percentage charge on each transaction if you are a seller accepting PayPal payments. To register on PayPal, log on to www.paypal.co.uk and fill out a 'sign up' form. You then choose between a personal account or a premier account in the country where you are located. A 'Personal Account' allows you to send payments to anyone with a personal email address and receive non-credit-card-funded payments. A 'Premier Account' allows you to both send payments and receive credit or debit card payments. A 'Business Account' allows you to send and receive payments under your business account.

- A registration form will then appear which asks for basic personal details and an email address. You are also asked if you require a Premier Account – you can upgrade to this account at a later date so just stick with the Personal Account for now.
- You will be asked for a password so try and use one that is different from your eBay password, especially as there is money involved with this site.

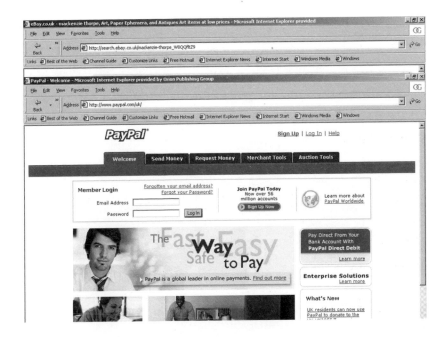

PayPal home page.

- A series of numbers and letters will appear which you will need to re-enter into a separate box as a form of confirmation and security before agreeing to the PayPal terms and conditions.
- Now you are fully signed-up for PayPal and an email is sent to you confirming registration.
- You will also be asked if you would like to register a credit or debit card – you do not have to do this but your account will have limitations on it if you don't.
- You will be now be able to receive money from other PayPal users.
- If you to choose to register a card with your account you need to enter all the relevant details. PayPal will then make two small withdrawals from that card to ensure you are the owner. These amounts will appear on your next card state-

ment – you then log into 'verify account' and put in the amounts that were deducted. Again an email will be sent confirming your PayPal account is active.

- The only account that you can both send and receive credit cards payments from is a Premier Account, to which you can upgrade at any time. You will not be charged a fee to upgrade to the Premier Account but you will have to pay between 1.9% + 20p and 3.4% + 20p for each transaction.

- Once you are fully registered you can then start buying and selling, making payments through PayPal. If you have a balance in the account then PayPal will take payment for goods from this first before deducting from your registered card.

- You are also able to withdraw your funds to a bank account. To do this you have to follow certain instructions with PayPal, including setting up a direct debit – this is to prove that you are the legitimate owner of the bank account. As with the credit-card system, once you have entered your bank details PayPal will deposit two very small amounts into your account, which you then have to verify with PayPal to prove it is your bank account.

- The money you have made sits in your account until you purchase something with it or are ready to move any funds to your bank account. This is simple and it takes 5–7 days for the money to hit your bank account. You simply press 'Withdraw' and you will then be asked to type in how much – you are allowed to withdraw anything over £50 free; for anything under £49.99 a fee of 25p is deducted.

- You are able to add or remove a credit card, email address or personal details at any time through your profile.

- PayPal is also secure for a buyer as they have a 'charge back' policy. If the seller has not been reliable and sent the item or there are other problems then the buyer can claim their money back if the seller's account is solvent. However, bear in mind that under new international money-laundering laws PayPal now has a policy that once your PayPal account has £5,000+ in it, you will be asked to make contact. Click on 'call now' and you will then receive a phone call, which will give you a number or code. You then enter this code into your PayPal account.

Top tip: Vic Jelenski says, 'I prefer payment by cheque so I can manage my accounts well. PayPal is a good form of payment but there is commission to be paid and it takes time for the money to come through and hit your account anyway so a cheque is just as good and many buyers prefer simply writing and sending a cheque rather than using the whole online payment thing. Good old-fashioned postal orders are another great form of payment as anyone can get these with cash and it's more secure than sending cash – I find those without bank accounts prefer this option. I won't take money orders though, either from the UK and certainly not abroad, as the charges levied by UK banks to accept these are huge. American money orders can cost £30 to put through your bank account.'

POSTAGE FEES

Now that you have sold your item here's the labour-intensive bit. In reality, it's likely that plenty of bidders or potential bidders will have been in touch with you to get an idea of postage, but if you have not yet assessed this cost then:

Take the item the Post Office to be properly weighed and priced for postage – bearing in mind that the postage may increase if a lot of wrapping or a heavy box is used.

Consider investing in a good set of scales that will allow you to calculate accurately the weight of the item.

Once the weight is known, visit www.royalmail.co.uk, as this website outlines all the various options for posting and the costs per weight. Alternatively, you can get a booklet from your local Post Office.

The buyer will send you the postage cost along with the final auction amount. If it is an expensive item then 'Special Delivery' is recommended as it is fully insured and guarantees next-day delivery.

Alternatively, use 'Recorded Delivery' which insures items up to £28 but does not necessarily guarantee that the buyer will receive them the next day.

There are other options for sending items, including 'Parcel Force' or 'Standard Parcel'. This is another service that is given at the Post Office, especially if the item is big and bulky then 'Standard Parcel' is a lot cheaper and is still insured.

If the parcel does not arrive at its destination, or is lost in transit, but is insured then contact the Post Office to claim a refund.

> **Top tip:** I usually refund the buyer first and then claim my own refund through the Post Office. Alternatively, if the item is not insured and the buyer did not ask for insurance it is up to the discretion of the seller whether they give a full refund or not.

Make sure that this is perfectly clear on your listing, e.g. 'Should you choose not to pay insurance then I cannot offer a refund.' The same applies if the buyer is not happy with the item on arrival but you have described it correctly. If the buyer accuses you of not describing properly then you must offer a full refund on safe return of the item. Alternatively, a buyer may wish to save on postage so will ask to come and pick this item up from you personally, as long as you are OK with this then it should not be a problem for the buyer to do so.

PACKAGING

Obviously, how many items you are expecting to sell will determine how much packaging you need.

Allow for packaging costs. You can seek out a supplier that sells flat-pack boxes and jiffy bags really cheaply. Check out your *Yellow Pages* or the Internet for packaging companies.

Don't forget to pack out your items within the box, especially if they are fragile, i.e. china or glass items. Newspaper helps but can make excess weight and, of course, this makes the cost of packaging higher.

Polystyrene chips are probably the best, as they are very protective and very light, while bubble wrap is a great way to package – and don't forget fragile or brown parcel tape to seal the package.

Brown parcel tape is best as it is designed with cardboard boxes in mind. Whatever you use, do not use ordinary Sellotape as this may easily come undone during carriage, especially if the parcel gets slightly damp in a warehouse. Both parcel tape and polystyrene chips can be bought at any main packaging supplier.

Take into consideration the amount of packaging that you use, as all these costs add up and should be included in the final postage costs quoted to the buyer.

Top tip: If you cannot afford at first to purchase packaging from a supplier then ask at your local supermarket. They will be only too happy to save boxes for you if you ask. Also consider approaching department stores or specialist china retailers, who may also be prepared to save chips and bubble wrap for you to pick up and use again.

FEEDBACK

This is the system designed to show other eBayers that you are a reliable and trustworthy seller or buyer. A crucial aspect of eBay is its self-policing system, which relies totally on eBay buyers and sellers using – in a responsible manner – the feedback facilities. So:

Once the transaction is complete both buyer and seller leave each other a message to tell other eBayers what they thought of your service.

This is simply done by clicking on the 'feedback forum' at the bottom of the home page. This then takes you into a screen to leave feedback and you have a choice of leaving either positive, neutral or negative feedback.

Having chosen which you want to leave and typed the message, e.g. 'Good eBayer, fast payment, a credit to eBay', hit the 'leave feedback' button.

If leaving neutral or negative feedback think carefully because once you have registered this feedback it cannot be altered. However, the buyer has the option to answer your comments on his or her own feedback for others to read and decide for themselves.

Whether feedback left is negative, positive or neutral will affect your overall feedback rating as an eBay seller.

Once you hit a feedback rating of ten a yellow star appears next to your user name and then as you gain more positive feedback the star will change colour to show that you are a reliable and honest dealer.

Positive gains you one feedback rating, negative loses you one and neutral leaves the score the same, although other eBayers can see that you have a neutral. This ensures that the whole eBay system works for all involved. Should someone have a lot of negative feedback then you know to give them a wide berth.

> *Top tip:* Vic Jelenski suggests, 'Never leave feedback until the buyer has left it for you. This way you know that the buyer has completed the sale and is happy. As you can only leave your feedback comments once, you don't want to leave positive feedback only to find that the buyer was dissatisfied with the sale and leaves you negative feedback in return.'

A PROBLEM WITH YOUR AUCTION?

Not all auctions run smoothly, especially when people fail to pay for the items that they have won or they insist that they never received the parcel. Even Jamie Oliver has had problems when he listed one of his scooters for sale on the site and found someone had bid £1m for the Aprilla two-wheeler. As the chef suspected, the bid was a hoax, but he still managed to get £25,000 for the vehicle and raise a further £7,000 from eBay itself towards his 'Cheeky Chops' charity. For everyone else, though, try to:

Deal with any problems amicably with the buyer by sending emails and trying to sort the problem out between yourselves.

If this does not work use eBay's www.squaretrade.com system, which helps sellers who have an online dispute that they would like resolved. It offers the chance for the traders to attempt to sort out their differences through a web-based forum or, if things do become difficult, you can opt for a professional mediator. You can file a case free of charge, then Square Trade informs the other party about your complaint by email. Once both parties involved are aware of the issues they source to find agreement and resolve the matter. All of this is coordinated by email but should the parties still fail to come to an amicable decision then, at a cost, a professional mediator can get involved and try to resolve the matter by offering suggestions to both parties.

Top tip: Vic Jelenski suggests, 'If there is a problem and an item needs to be returned to you, remember to reimburse the buyer for their postage on top of the cost of the item per se. Most honest buyers who have such a problem are happy to provide you with proof of the cost of postage and you never know, this buyer may want to buy from you in future. You don't want to put them off bidding on your items as the more bidders the higher the potential auction result.'

SHORTCUTS

Once you have sold a few items and your confidence is growing then there are all sorts of options that can speed up the entire process of buying and selling on eBay. These include:

Listing by downloading 'Turbo Lister', which enables a seller to list lots of items that can then be uploaded onto eBay quickly and efficiently.

Log into www.ebay.co.uk and click Site Map > Seller Tools > Turbo Lister – Improved Bulk Upload Tool.

Exercise the option to download the programme, which is basically a Word document.

Every time you wish to sell something you go into this document and fill it out, much the same as the selling forms on eBay. The only difference is that all listed items stay on the document until you delete them and you can add as much as you like and then upload onto eBay at your leisure.

Once you have set up the template, every time you

visit Turbo Lister you can create a new listing from the template.

When you are ready to place the listed items on eBay you simply go into Turbo Lister and highlight the items that you want to sell and press the 'upload onto eBay' button. This calculates your listing fees and transfers the information straight to the website.

This system is a must for any seller who has mastered the art of selling and wants to list lots of items in one go. It is far less time-consuming than loading individual items through the eBay system itself.

Vic Jelenski has sold all sorts of things on ebay.co.uk and believes in constantly testing the market to see what demand there is for different items. For example he has sold:

• A 'Dan Dare' radio set in its box and dating from the 1950s/1960s for £78 – bought from a boot sale for £2.
• A 'Thomas the Tank Engine' collection of engines purchased at a boot sale as a job lot for £102, which were then sold individually on eBay for a total of £650.
• A collection of 160 unopened Airfix kits purchased as bankrupt stock from a model shop for £150 and sold in total for £830.
• A set of Homepride weights in the shape of 'Fred the Flourman' made £150 on eBay having been purchased at a boot sale in Essex last year for £3.

- A 1952 Subbuteo price list, which came as part of a Subbuteo game purchased at a boot sale for £2, made £80 on its own on eBay while the rest of the actual game made only £16.
- A Corgi 1970s Magic Roundabout toy bought for £80 at a boot sale in Kent realised £1,000 on ebay.co.uk.

Tracy Martin is a regular boot-saler and eBay seller and her finds and fortunes include:

- An Escada ladies' pinstripe suit purchased at a Southend-on-Sea, Essex, boot sale for £15, which made £395 on ebay.com thanks to auction fever. A further two Escada suits realised only £60 each – still a profit on the £40 the pair cost at another boot sale.
- A 1980s Vivienne Westwood skirt, which cost £1.50 at Stevenson's Farm, Essex, boot sale, made £65 on eBay.

The November 2004 issue of *Vogue* carried an article describing how one of its journalists raided the *Vogue* offices and listed the items found on eBay. Among the sales were:

- Three Matthew Williamson-designed limited-edition bottles of Coca Cola, which made £40.
- A copy each of *Vogue*'s Silver Millennium and Gold 2000 issues, which realised £25 the pair.
- A small Pucci paper bag, which made £3.80.
- A Fendi credit-card holder, which realised £14.50.

Martin Donovan has been selling on eBay regularly since 2002 and his sales include:

• A 2004 Harrods teddy bear purchased under the Harrods offer to all customers, which allowed them to buy three bears for the price of two. For an outlay of £49.90 he purchased three Harrods bears – one of which alone has made £41 on eBay. A further four Harrods Annual Bears bought at a boot sale for £90 have sold for £70 (Year 2000), £45 (Year 2001), £50 (Year 2002) and £70 (Year 2003).

Harrods Annual Bears are popular with collectors and increase in value. A 2004 bear recently sold on eBay for £41.

• A set of 'Magic Roundabout' badges produced in 1998 to raise funds for the Anthony Nolan Trust and bought at a boot sale for 50p realised £20 the set and there is even a website, www.charitybadges.com, dedicated to listing all the charity badges produced.

• A collection of 'Bob the Builder' character toys made under licence by Hit Entertainment were purchased at £2.49 each in a half-price offer at a department store in Upminster on a special account-holder day, which included a 10% additional discount for those with the department store's card. They realised £5–£18 each on eBay.

- A Christie's auction catalogue found in the loft from 1999 covering a Clarice Cliff sale and sent free to him because he had bought from the auction house before. This realised £68 on eBay.
- A Beswick Jay large bird figurine which was broken and re-glued in three places was bought for £2 from an Essex boot sale and realised £92 on eBay, while a Staffordshire flat-back figurine bought from a boot sale seller for £1 because the woman 'loathed it' made £198.

Paul Foster has been selling on eBay as a hobby for the past year or so. He has had many successes, which include:

- A 1997 Robert Harrop resin 'Dennis the Menace' plaque, which he paid £3 for at a car boot sale. This sold for £620 on ebay.co.uk as it is one of the rarest Robert Harrop pieces that collectors fight over.
- A Royal Doulton 'Highlander' Snowman figure, which he purchased from eBay for £150. When it arrived, he realised that it was missing the red colouring from its kilt, and after checking with one of the modellers at Royal

This Royal Doulton 'Highlander' Snowman was bought on ebay.co.uk for £150 and resold back on eBay for an amazing £800.

Doulton, it was confirmed to be an 'oddity' which had slipped through the net of the production line. He eventually resold it back onto eBay and it realised an amazing £800.

• A Cambridge-glass 1930s Flower Frog of Peter Pan and Tinkerbell. Bought for £80 from an antiques shop, this made £300 on ebay.com, which was amazing as it was not in the best condition, having some chips to the base of the frog.

• Also, with the television programme *Friends* ending last year, he bought a tin featuring the show, designed to look like a television set. Paying just £2 he was shocked when it sold for £35.

• A pair of modern children's 'Tom and Jerry' glove puppets bought for £1 each from two different boot sale stalls made £37.50 when sold on eBay.

Conclusion

• Always make sure your photographs and descriptions are as factually correct and complimentary about your items as you can.

• Never ignore problems or emails – but allow plenty of time to deal with these if you want to become a successful eBayer.

• Always be prepared to try different items on eBay until you find a particular area that proves successful.

• Make friends with the staff at your local post office as you will be seeing a lot of them, and take time to source wholesale companies for wrapping and boxes as this will save you a fortune in the long run compared to shop prices.

- Don't forget to provide feedback and try to avoid tit-for-tat bad feedback battles.

CHAPTER SEVEN

BUYING ON EBAY

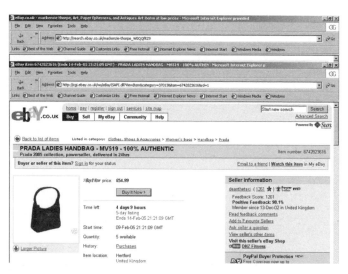

eBay 'Buy It Now' page.

Everyone has heard of someone buying an incredible bargain on eBay or bagging an item for half the price charged on the high street. But for every story of great finds on the Internet there are also warnings of disappointment, non-delivery, import taxes being levied on the doorstep and sellers who refuse to reimburse buyers' money. It's not surprising that there are some problems. After all, with any massively expanding business the odds are against every single purchase going smoothly. To give you an idea of the growth recorded to date, shopping on the Internet has soared by a third since 2003, with online purchases amounting to £6.4bn in 2004 with the most popular buys being CDs, DVDs, electronic goods and clothes.

Similarly, with a business that is expanding rapidly and self-policed for every 100 responsible sellers and buyers there is likely to be the odd bad apple. Just as boot sales were once wrongly slighted with a reputation of being a dumping ground for stolen goods so has this charge been levied against eBay. A mechanic who lost tools worth £350 in a burglary got them back on eBay. Tony Wilson from Warminster in Wiltshire out-bid everyone attempting to buy his tools, which he found listed on the site. He passed on the seller's details to police, who investigated, only to be told that the seller had purchased the lot at a boot sale. However, when Allan Macpherson-Fletcher found his Scottish country home had been broken into last year, he realised the thieves had got away with his £10,000 eighteenth- and nineteenth-century collection of Meissen, Worcester and Sevres china. On the advice of friends he checked the eBay site and found a familiar-looking plate. When he then checked the seller's other listings 'jolly well nearly the whole china cabinet came up'. Getting a relative to bid on the items on his behalf, he bought the entire collection back, bar one piece on which he was outbid. The items he purchased included a Meissen plate at £14.95 and a figurine at £255; both were worth far more than this. On completion of the auctions, the seller promptly emailed his details to Mr Macpherson-Fletcher, who in turn handed the information over to the police. A man was arrested and eighteen of the twenty-six stolen items were recovered. The man in question has been charged with handling stolen property, although the police are convinced the same person did not actually commit the original break-in.

It's not just stolen goods that can be relatively easy to offload via the eBay site. There are plenty of cases of straightforward fraud. eBay acts swiftly wherever there is good cause to suspect a fraud taking place and works closely with the authorities to address the problem, but usually the crime has already taken place before the fraud is uncovered. There have been several court cases in the UK where individuals have been jailed for running scams on the eBay website. Business studies university student Michael Broughton, twenty-three, and his best friend, IT worker Paul Wilson, twenty-two, offered Prada shoes, Gucci luggage and Louis Vuitton bags up on ebay.com. They took the cash from the 'sale' of each item using aliases to set up the accounts and then spent it on holidays. In December 2004, at Sheffield Crown Court, the pair were each jailed for nine months for fraud. Interestingly, Andrew Woolfson, defending the pair, said, 'It seemed like an easy way to make money but was always a harebrained scheme.' Unfortunately, this is of little consolation to those who were hit by the pair's fraud. Obviously, ebay.com cannot be held responsible for such events, but as the popularity of the auction website grows, the likelihood of such scams happening will increase too. This is why the age-old adage of 'buyer beware' applies as much today as it has always done within the traditional auction houses.

Common sense should prevail at all times and if in doubt check, check and check again, either by emailing the seller or emailing eBay itself. If you have serious doubts, my advice would be better safe than sorry. Bearing all this in mind, there's no doubt that eBay is the biggest boot sale of them all, with millions of items available, thousands of bargains to be had and hundreds of transactions between buyers and sellers taking place every hour, all of which proceed to everyone's all-round satisfaction. So, how do you start buying from this enormous worldwide shop window?

The events of 11 September 2001 may have shocked the world but the tragedy also revealed a darker side to the collecting market and human nature, as several listings appeared on ebay.com offering dust and remnants of the Twin Towers for sale. All were swiftly removed by eBay and a temporary ban was put on anything that covered the Twin Towers or the Pentagon during or after the attacks. However, when Brighton Pier caught fire and was effectively destroyed, salvagers started listing the debris that washed up on Brighton beach. Fortunately, no one was killed in this incident but nevertheless the loss of such an historic building brings into question the moral legitimacy of selling such 'memorabilia' on the Internet. The vast majority of people, however, are no different to Cherie Blair, the Prime Minister's wife. She may earn a reported £250,000 a year (okay, that bit is different from the rest of us) but she's still an eBay bargain hunter. Her purchases include a children's alarm clock for son Leo (which caused concern when it was sent by the eBay seller to 10 Downing Street ticking away). She also bought a pair of vintage red shoes worth £100 that cost £10 on the auction site.

To start your own search for an eBay bargain:

Go online and type www.ebay.com into your online provider's address bar.

You will arrive at the home page of the worldwide eBay website.

Whatever you want to know can be found by working your way around the home page and back again.

Using the home page search engine, type in the item or

items that you are interested in, making sure you have used the correct spelling.

Any items on eBay that are currently being auctioned and fit your item description will come up – to check out UK-only items go to www.ebay.co.uk. This will automatically show items available only in the UK.

The item being auctioned will include the current bidding price, a full description of the piece, the seller's details and more often than not a photograph.

By using the computer's forward and back buttons you can review as many items from the current auction listings as possible.

Often the same items will appear but with a different level of bidding activity, so it's worth checking the descriptions to see why one item may have a single bid yet another identical piece has 100 bidders fighting over it.

If you wish to search for something else then simply go back to the www.ebay.co.uk home page and click on 'item worldwide'.

Don't just search ebay.com: it's usually a good idea to stick to the ebay.co.uk site for your first purchases as the whole bidding and transaction process is less complicated buying from your own country.

Remember you are only able to browse at this stage, not bid.

On the left-hand side of each eBay main item listings a box can be found which includes the words 'completed items'. If you click on this the listings will be refreshed with all the items that match your original description but have already been sold.

> *Top tip:* Bear in mind that there can be descriptive variations on items – for example, Americans tend to call handbags 'purses' and refer to plastic items as 'lucite', while Lenci as an item description will bring up both Lenci dolls and Lenci figurines.

How do eBay Auctions Work?

There are different types of auctions available to sellers on eBay and it's vital that you read each individual seller's auction description carefully so that you fully understand how the seller is auctioning the piece – and that you do this before you bid. Generally, the most common is a straightforward listing that offers an item for sale over a set period of time. The closing time for each auction is listed both in date and time, and in terms of how many days or hours and minutes the item has to run before the 'hammer comes down'. Remember:

To register with eBay you must have a working email address. These are simple to set up and many Internet sites offer free email services. Find a site such as Yahoo or Hotmail supplying this free service and follow the easy instructions to obtain your email address. Make sure that you keep a note of your address and the password otherwise you will have to re-register another one. Once you have obtained your email address you are ready to click into www.ebay.co.uk and register.

Once you have opened up www.ebay.co.uk, you will be confronted with a home page and at the very top is the word 'register'. Click onto this and it will take you into a form that needs to be completed in order to start the registration process. On completion you will then be asked to read and agree the 'user agreement'. Once this is completed you then click the relevant boxes to prove that you have done so and click 'continue'.

Next you will need to get an eBay user name, which is your own unique ID within the eBay world. eBay itself provides you with some options that you can choose or if you prefer you can think up one of your own. Choose carefully and keep a separate note of your ID on paper in your home in case you forget it. This is effectively the same as a traditional auction house's paddle or bidding number, which is given to you once you register at an auction house – except in the case of eBay your ID will be the same whatever auction you bid on.

The next step is to create a password. Try not to use the same password as applies to your email address in order to prevent others gaining access without your knowledge. You will then be asked to enter a 'secret question' and 'secret answer'. This again is to ensure that the site remains secure and only you will know the answers. Once you have completed these steps then you click 'continue', which takes you onto the final page. A confirmation email is sent to your email address and this has a registration code. You click onto 'complete eBay registration'. This confirms with eBay that your email is valid and you then become a fully-fledged member of the eBay community.

> *Top tip:* eBay is very aware of the scams and tricks that go on and will never email you asking for personal details, account details or personal pin numbers to be revealed. As with any email that asks for such information, extreme caution must be taken or you can easily find your bank and credit accounts being cloned or used fraudulently. I always contact my bank and credit-card issuers directly if I am sent such emails and only deal with such requests direct by phone, when certain extra passwords and codes can be used to ensure that your accounts remain secure. eBay has recently launched 'My Messages', which will come up on your 'My eBay' page when you register on the site each time.

Ready to Bid on eBay?

So you've registered, and you're up, running and raring to go and bid on an item that you have seen listed. Remain calm and don't forget common sense. Don't be tempted to get carried away in the excitement of it all and bid straight away. Take care to read the seller's description in full, taking note of the following:

The condition of the item on which you are going to bid. Is there any damage, chips, flaking, pieces missing, etc? Some sellers can waffle on, while others provide the most scant of details

– if you have any queries about the condition that are not answered in the seller's description, email the seller directly. This can be done by clicking on the appropriate link on the seller's page.

The postage and packaging costs for sending the piece to you, as certain sellers may waive the packaging costs but not have listed the potential postage charges. Others insist on sending every item they sell using a certain level of service, such as registered post or Parcel Force. They have the right to insist on this but if you have a sensible alternative, it can be worth proposing this to the seller. If you have any queries, email the seller and wait for his or her reply before you bid. The minute you bid you are not only bidding on the item but also accepting the seller's terms of auction.

What type of auction is being offered and make sure that you understand how this particular type of auction works. By going back to the eBay home page and clicking on eBay's own descriptions of auction types you will find the information you need.

Where in the country the item is, if collection is required and work out whether it is feasible for you to collect the item should you be the winning bidder.

Any starting bid indicated in the seller's auction box. This will be the price at which the seller wishes to start the auction and if no one makes a bid at this price, the auction will remain listed as active for the duration indicated on the listing but the item sale will not actually complete. Any reserve will be concealed. The listing will indicate 'reserve not met' but will not reveal what the reserve is. This can be frustrating and result in potential buyers making lots of bids at an increasing amount to try and hit the reserve. Bear in mind that if you do hit the reserve, your bid is real and active and, if no one outbids you, the obligation is on you to complete the sale, so make sure you are not bidding beyond your financial means. Email the seller asking what the reserve on the piece is, as many will let you know the figure although they are not obliged to do so. Alternatively, email the seller with the proposed price you are prepared to go to, asking whether this would beat the reserve and at least then you know whether you are in with a chance or nowhere near the seller's required sum.

The seller's feedback rating, which can be checked by clicking on the rating indicated on the listing. Bear in mind that new sellers will not have much if any feedback. You want to see positive feedback and responses that indicate from past buyers that the transaction has run smoothly and that any problems have been professionally taken care of.

The seller's requested payment terms. These can range from PayPal payments only to cheques only and you must adhere to these requests. If you wish to propose an alternative you need to email the seller before bidding and get the seller's agreement ahead of time.

Any seller's insurance requirement. You can be expected to pay this charge, which protects the seller should the item arrived damaged. Most postal services offer some type of insurance cover at an extra cost so it's straightforward.

Remember you will be required to leave feedback for the seller if your bid is successful but equally the seller will be leaving feedback about you on your own buyer's listing so take an objective and professional view when assessing a seller's feedback rating. Feedback is a crucial aspect of eBay as sellers do not always like dealing with people who have a low feedback score or, in the case of a first-time bidder, no feedback at all. The more communication you have with the seller on a professional basis the more the seller is likely to have faith that you will proceed with the transaction. The more you buy and the more you proceed with smooth purchases the more your own feedback rating will rise and the less suspicious sellers become.

Some sellers will indicate that they will be away and unable to answer emails until a set date, which might be after the auction has finished; others may encourage you to check out their other items listed or invite you to email requests for further pictures if required. Increasingly, sellers are making it clear on their listings that they pack and post only on a set day of the week, so if the auction ends on a Saturday they may say they pack and post on Fridays only. You will need to bear all this in mind if you are in a rush to get the piece.

Top tip: www.fatfingers.co.uk is a really innovative website, which is easy to use and can help you find loads of bargains on eBay. You simply log in and type what you are looking for then press the 'generate' button. A yellow box appears at the bottom of the page which reads 'click here to find misspellings on ebay.co.uk'. You click onto this and it takes you into the eBay listings of everything that is spelt incorrectly for the particular item or brand that you are looking for. You can then just browse and bid as normal. You can end up bagging some real bargains as people are not always aware that these items are listed.

eBay auction page.

Time to Bid

Only when you have fully considered everything above are you in a position to decide whether you wish to go ahead and bid on the item. Assuming you do, click on the 'Place Bid' button. This will take you to another page which requests your eBay user ID and password. Fill this in and press 'sign in securely'. You will be taken to another page where you place your bid. Check that the item title is correct and matches the piece you plan to bid for and check out the current bid price. This is the price at which the bid currently stands. Then enter the price you want to pay but remember:

 Decide on the maximum price you are willing to pay and

stick to this, taking into account postage costs and any other charges that may be levied for insurance, delivery and even your credit-card charges or interest should the seller request payment this way. Money orders and postal orders both mean charges, although a personal cheque drawn against a personal account or paying through PayPal will be free of charge.

eBay itself does not charge a commission on the hammer price to the buyer. Traditional auctions will charge a percentage of the hammer price to both the buyer and the seller but the joy of eBay is that you can buy, buy, buy without paying commission to the auctioneer – eBay.

If insurance is not offered but the piece is valuable then you may wish to get the item insured for delivery anyway and most sellers can accommodate this but would probably like to know that you wish this to be the case ahead of the auction ending.

Once your bid has been placed you will be asked to confirm it, and once this is done you will receive an automatic message acknowledging your bid and indicating that you are the successful bidder.

Your bid may not be accepted if it is under the current bid or not sufficiently higher than the current bid in which case the return message will indicate the minimum amount you will have to bid in order to become the successful bidder.

If you bid considerably more than the current bid the return message may indicate your bid is successful at considerably less than you are willing to pay because eBay bids for you in rising increments until you are the highest bidder. A new bidder may bid but until they top the amount you originally put in, their bid will not be successful.

Your return message may read that your bid has been successful but at the maximum amount you originally bid. Be careful here, as you can easily be outbid because there is no more flexibility left in the original bid for eBay to increase it on your behalf. Consider increasing your bid immediately or make sure you opt to list this auction in 'auctions I am watching', taking a note of when the auction is ending so that you can log on again at this time and increase your bid.

If your bid is successful the price of the current bid will be revealed on the seller's listings page along with your eBay user ID.

There are plenty of stories of people staying up all night to bid on items, but with the eBay tools on offer this is not necessary if you have deep pockets and don't care what you pay. You simply bid a ridiculous amount to secure it, which ensures that no one can outbid you. However, staying up and bidding as an auction ends can also result in the 'auction fever' first recognised in traditional auction rooms, where individuals find the item takes on a personality all of its own. Rational human beings can suddenly find themselves bidding beyond their means, or beyond the true value of an item, just to secure it and stop someone else from getting it. The euphoria quickly subsides once the bill comes in and if you fear you have a susceptibility to auction fever, make your bid ahead of time and then leave well alone.

Top tip: Reilly Carver, eBay enthusiast, suggests 'I learned pretty quickly not to bid early because if someone else wants the item then the price can be pushed up as you try to outbid each other. I was caught out several times in this way when buying pieces for an old dinner service I am collecting. Now, if I see an item I want I put it into my watch file, decide the maximum I am prepared to pay and put the bid in with a minute or less to go to the deadline. It usually works. I bought a four-poster bed in this way a few months ago and got it far cheaper than they usually go for on eBay. There were two other bidders. The price started around £600 and had reached £1,200. I went in at the end with £1,500 and got it for £1,260 as the highest previous bid was £1,250. I reckon if I had gone in earlier I would have entered a bidding war and it would have passed the £2,000 mark.'

For those of you who are continually losing out to last-minute bidders on eBay, check out www.auctionsniper.com. You place a bid with the sniper. As with eBay, type in the highest price that you are willing to pay. Then in the last few seconds before the auction closes Sniper will make the bid for you and nine times out of ten you will win the object that you desperately wanted. If you sign up and register with Auction Sniper then your first three winning snipes are free. After you have used these free snipes there is a charge of 1% on the final purchase price of further winning bids. This is a site worth registering on if an auction finishes in the middle of the night or you desperately want to win something.

'Buy It Now' Bids

A seller may have incorporated a 'Buy It Now' option into their auction. This indicates the price at which the seller is willing to sell their item. This allows a buyer to either place a bid or buy the item outright. This option is available only when there are no bids placed and where a single item is listed (but see Fixed-Price Auction on page 201).

You can search eBay to find the 'Buy It Now' items by clicking on search as all auctions offering this service will feature the 'Buy It Now' icon alongside the listing. Alternatively, you can click onto the 'Buy It Now' tab which will list only those auctions offering this facility.

eBay 'Buy It Now' page.

Before buying using this process, make sure that you take into consideration the following:

Check all 'Buy It Now' prices. Some sellers offer an item cheaper and you still want to get a bargain.

You can narrow down your search by checking only 'Buy It Now' sellers and asking for the lowest price on the drop-down menu.

Check whether the seller accepts only PayPal or alternative methods of payment and whether they require you to pay for the item immediately.

Ensure that the seller has included all postage and insurance costs with the final price.

Click on the 'Buy It Now' button on the auction listing page.

If asked for immediate payment click 'continue to PayPal' and then complete the payment process.

Payment will then be confirmed and the item is now yours.

If the 'Buy It Now' option is used by a buyer then the auction will automatically come to an end. If a bid has come in first then the 'Buy It Now' option will disappear (unless the item also has a reserve, in which case the 'Buy It Now' will disappear only if the reserve price is met). In both these cases the auction will carry out its duration.

Top tip: You will need to complete the payment process quickly if you wish to purchase an item outright, as another buyer can come in and purchase it, completing the process quicker and snapping the item up before you have had a chance to buy it.

Fixed-Price Auction

This is when there is no normal auction format. Bidding is just by 'Buy It Now' option. This allows the seller to set the price that they want for an item in the hope that it will sell quickly and they won't have to wait for an auction to finish. Buyers can then just purchase the item outright. Sellers can also sell multiple items using this process and the 'Buy It Now' icon does not disappear once an item from multiple listings has been purchased.

A seller has to have a minimum feedback rating of ten or have placed direct-debit details on file to use this fixed-price format.

It gives buyers the opportunity to purchase an item straight away.

The same system of purchasing as for 'Buy It Now' auctions is used. Click: Buy It Now > Enter Quantity To Purchase > Continue > Purchase Item.

Dutch (Multiple-Item) Auction

A multiple-item auction, otherwise known as a Dutch auction, is when a seller has one or more identical items to sell. When bidding on these auctions you have to specify the number of items that you would like to buy and the price you are willing to pay. The seller does indicate a starting price, just as in a usual auction format, and this is usually what a buyer will pay.

All winning bidders will pay the same price at the end of the auction duration.

Unlike normal auctions, the price is the lowest successful bid rather than the highest.

Normally the price paid is the starting price but if there are more bids than items, the winning buyers will be the ones that placed the earliest successful bid.

In order to beat a bid you must have placed a higher total bid per item. This is regardless of how many items you have placed bids on. For example:

There are twenty items available to bid on:
Bidder 1 has bid for ten items at £10 each
Bidder 2 has bid for eleven items at £11 each.

In this example the lowest successful bid is Bidder 1 for £10.
So the result is:
Bidder 2 wins eleven items at £11 each
Bidder 1 wins nine items at £10 each.

This auction allows a winning bidder to refuse partial quantities. So, for example, if a bidder wanted five items and won only four, they do not have to buy any of the items if they do not wish to do so.

Live Auction Bids

This is the most common format used by sellers on the eBay site. The seller has chosen a duration of either one, three, five, seven or ten days for which to list their item, with a starting price. If, as a buyer, you want to place a bid then you simply do the following:

Search eBay to find an item that you are interested in buying.

Check the description to make sure that you are happy with the item that is being sold.

Read additional costs such as postage, etc to make sure that it falls within the price you want to pay in total.

Work out whether you want to place a bid straight away or wait until nearer the end of the auction – make sure you make a note of when the auction finishes.

See how many bids have already been left and browse completed items to get an idea of what price the item might sell for or has sold for in the past.

When you are happy with the item and description press 'Place a Bid' on the seller's page.

Enter the highest amount that you are willing to pay.

If the starting price is 99p and no one else has placed a bid then even though you may have bid £5 the item will sit at 99p, with you as the highest bidder, until someone else places a bid. If no one bids against you during the auction then you will win the item for the starting price of 99p.

Your bidding increases as 'Proxy Bids', i.e. your 99p will increase if another person bids between £1.00 and £4.99, so that you will automatically outbid that person. Only when a rival bidder has entered £5.01 or more will you be outbid altogether.

Reserve Price Auction

 A reserve price is the minimum price that a seller is willing to accept for his item.

 A buyer is unable to see the reserve price until it is met by a buyer.

 A seller does not have to sell the item if his reserve price is not met.

 To win the item you need to have placed a bid that is the same as the reserve price or higher.

 The seller's page will indicate in red next to the current auction price if the 'reserve not yet met' or in blue if the 'reserve met'.

Private Auction

 A seller may choose to keep their auction private, which

means that the user IDs of bidders are not displayed on the listing.

The seller is able to see the ID only of the highest bidder during the auction and only the winning bidder's ID once the auction has finished.

During the Auction

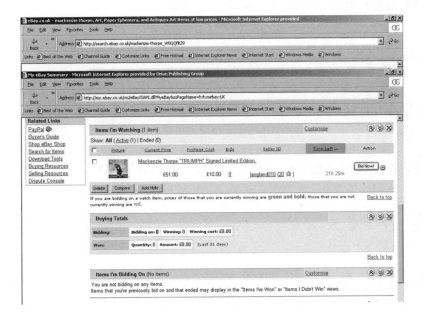

'My eBay' watching page.

Once you have placed a successful bid the seller's auction page will automatically be placed onto your 'My eBay' section under 'Bidding'. If you haven't placed a bid but are interested in the item, you can click on 'Watch this Item' on the seller's page and it will again be placed onto 'My eBay' under 'Watching'. This is a great facility, which allows you to keep an eye on as many auctions as you care to watch. The 'My eBay' page is an option that comes each time you log into the eBay site. The 'My eBay' page also offers buyers the chance to:

Get notification automatically from eBay when an auction is completed and details of other similar items coming online to be auctioned.

Organise your own personal filing system to your own preference according to what you have bought and what you are interested in.

Get reminders of those sellers to whom you need to send payment.

Be provided with a running total of how much money you have already spent on successful purchases and how much you are spending currently, even though the auctions have yet to complete! No wonder this is at the bottom of the 'My eBay' page.

Check official ebay.com announcements.

Click directly through to paypal.com to send payments.

Link directly to the ebay.co.uk community pages, which are great forums for discussing purchases or problems with other UK eBay buyers and sellers.

Try out 'Want It Now' if you are desperately seeking a particular item, as this means all eBay sellers get notification and hopefully match you with someone who has the piece.

Use 'Favourite Searches', which automatically picks up and eases the process of searching for particular items. This is most useful if you are a collector of one or two particular collectables and regularly search for a certain item or items.

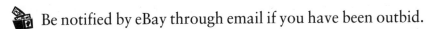 Access the official eBay currency converter, which is a great help if you start to buy internationally rather than just from the UK.

Be notified by eBay through email if you have been outbid.

Receive bid and buy alerts by mobile phone, although you will need to check with your individual mobile-phone provider what the charges for receiving these may be.

> *Top tip:* Reilly Carver explains, 'Just before Christmas I needed a kitchen table and decided to look at eBay. There were lots to chose from. Then I saw an ad for a new one. On reading details, the seller said he could make a table to order at any size. I wanted a five-foot-square table. I emailed him and asked if he could do it and within ten days I had the table, which is beautifully made and cost just £250. I was so thrilled with it I emailed the seller – who is actually the wife of the carpenter who made the table – to say how brilliant it was. As a result she says I have given her husband the confidence to make loads more and he now has an order for a twelve-foot table from France.'

Congratulations! You Won the Item

This means just that. You will receive an email telling you the final price and giving details of the seller. The sellers themselves may also send you confirmation and an automated page of the seller's details, required payment method and address. Remember:

You must reply to the email within three working days unless you have notified the seller and the seller has agreed to a delay because you will be away or unable to access a computer. If you have not made this agreement beforehand the seller may take the view that you do not plan to complete the sale and leave negative feedback about you.

You need to already have the payment method sorted so that if a personal cheque is required, your chequebook has not run out, as it can take ten days to get a new one. If a postal order is required bear in mind that these will cost, and allow plenty of time to buy the postal order and send it. If payment is being made by post through either of these methods then make sure you send it first class for swift delivery. Include a print-out or covering note with your address, the item number and the amount, so that the seller – who may be completing hundreds of transactions a week – knows exactly what you are paying for.

The seller will expect to bank the money and has an obligation to send the item out to you within ten days, unless you have both agreed otherwise. Bear in mind that if the item is being sent registered or recorded you have to sign for it. You will need to be at home to receive it and if not the postman should leave you a card asking you to pick up the item from your local Post Office.

If you are happy with the service and the item then leave the seller positive feedback.

Paying for your Item

PAYPAL

Before bidding for your item you will have read the seller's terms and conditions and know their required method of payment or will have emailed and confirmed the way in which you will be paying for the item. The majority of sellers will accept and often prefer PayPal, which is a service that is both quick, secure, reliable and free to buyers. It's worthwhile setting up a PayPal account even before you make your first bid and you can do this by completing a straightforward form, which is totally secure. Register by logging onto www.paypal.com, and fill out the 'Sign Up' form; there is no charge for this.

How do I deposit some money into my PayPal account?

Either set up a direct debit, which then enables you to add funds to your PayPal account straight from your UK bank account, or register a credit card from which payment can be deducted. On your bank statement two small deposits are made by PayPal. The exact amounts need to be added to your PayPal account to finish the verification process. Your bank account or credit card will then have two small deductions made by PayPal, which again are the verification codes that need to be placed onto your PayPal account. This is to prove that you are the account owner.

How long do I have to wait for the funds to credit my PayPal account?

Your bank account or credit card needs to be verified to prove that you are the owner. This can take up to a week. So if you intend to buy on eBay it might be a good idea to register with PayPal before you start bidding on items.

How do I settle my account with a seller?

When the auction has finished you can pay by pressing 'Pay Now' on your 'My eBay' page. This takes you straight to PayPal where you log in and complete payment as instructed.

How do I monitor my purchases?

Go to www.paypal.com and you will automatically be taken to your account page. You can see all the transactions for the last week, both money going in and money going out to sellers.

How do I change my payment method if my card expires or I wish to add a different card?

Clicking on 'My Profile' in PayPal, you can add or remove the card details. You will have to complete the verification process again. The amounts that PayPal deduct will appear on your next statement or if you bank online they will show as transactions made through your account. Allow a couple of days if you have online access and up to a month if you are waiting for your next card statement to arrive.

Can I set up more than one account if necessary?

It is possible to set up another PayPal account but you will need a different email address, bank account and/or credit card.

What happens once I have paid a seller?

Payment can be sent via eBay or from your PayPal account. If you have the seller's email address PayPal acknowledge payment sent by sending you a confirmation email. It also appears on your PayPal account page.

How long does it take for the seller to receive my payment?

Once payment is sent to the seller it credits their PayPal account immediately. Buyer and seller receive confirmation emails.

Can I get my money back if something goes wrong?

PayPal has a charge-back policy: if the seller proves unreliable or fails to send the item the buyer can claim their money back. This only applies if the seller's account is solvent.

What insurance does PayPal offer?

PayPal Buyer Protection covers buyers who never received the item they purchased or if the item is significantly different than described. Protection is only offered up to the value of £500 if:

 You file a claim within thirty days of the transaction.

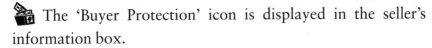 The 'Buyer Protection' icon is displayed in the seller's information box.

 The item is physical, not a service.

POSTAL ORDERS

Many UK buyers will accept UK Post Office postal orders – a convenient and cheap way to send money and available at all

UK Post Offices. This is the way to pay for your eBay goods if you do not have a bank account, as you can pay cash over the Post Office counter. Postal orders:

 Come in denominations of 50p–£20.00

 Can have stamps added to make up the odd amount such as £1.95

 Costs and charges are:

50p or £1	25p
£2, £3, £4	50p
£5, £6, £7	80p
£8, £9, £10	£1.05
£15	£1.15
£20	£1.25

> *Top tip:* You have to buy postal orders in person; there's no online facility for these purchases so save yourself time by avoiding the Post Office on pension day, i.e. Thursdays when queues can be very long. Visit the official Post Office website on www.postoffice.co.uk or call the helpline on 08457 223344 for further information.

CHEQUES

Not all UK eBay sellers have bank accounts and this can be a legitimate reason for requesting postal orders and refusing cheques. Most do accept UK cheques but cheques can take up to five working days to clear. Remember:

Complete the cheque legibly, including the correct date and year, and don't forget to sign it.

Add your cheque guarantee card details on the reverse of the cheque but remember that as the seller has not witnessed this, or checked your card, the seller may insist on full clearance before sending an item.

Do not write a cheque to anyone other than the seller or leave the cheque containing only your signature.

Send cheques first class unless the seller is prepared to wait for second-class delivery.

There should be no charge for the cheque to be processed through a personal bank account unless you have a particular type of foreign bank account, premier bank account or are using a company cheque.

You must have the funds or an approved overdraft for the cheque to clear.

If the cheque 'bounces' on the seller, they are entitled to withdraw from the sale and note this in the feedback they leave. They may well re-present the cheque but there will be a charge to the seller and to you for the cheque bouncing. The seller may seek to recover this charge from you.

CASH

Please don't send cash in the post no matter what the seller says. Sending cash, whether by registered or recorded post, is no guarantee that the cash itself will arrive. Furthermore, unscrupulous sellers can easily claim that the cash never arrived even if it did.

MONEY ORDERS

Most UK eBayers steer well clear of money orders as they cost money to deposit into a seller's bank account and this will in turn cut into the profit or increase the loss they make when selling the item. They are frequently requested by international sellers but you need to remember that an international money order:

 will involve a currency exchange and you will have to accept the rate set by the bank that you use to buy the money order – this may not be the most advantageous exchange rate, thus increasing the purchase price of the item.

 has to be pre-ordered and pre-paid at a bank and then picked up, which is a process that can take anything up to a week.

 is effectively cash allowing a seller to bank it in his or her country without you having any proof that this has been done.

 can only be traced leaving the country; there is no tracking system for you to know that it has been received or hit the seller's personal bank account.

 can get lost in transit and you have no means of reclaiming the money because it is effectively the same as cash going missing, even though you can prove it was drawn down on your own bank account.

 can cost up to £30 a time, which makes it an extremely expensive method of payment and increases the cost of the item purchased.

 will take considerable time to reach its destination.

BANKER'S DRAFT

Most banks can provide a UK banker's draft, which is effectively a piece of paper that has a face value dictated by you. In turn this means that you have to have provided the funds to the bank and the bank has debited the funds declared on the draft. A banker's draft is as good as cash and is normally best used when dealing with high-value transactions.

What is a banker's draft?

A banker's draft looks like a cheque but is drawn under a bank's head office rather than an individual person.

There are two different types: for UK transactions a 'sterling draft' and for overseas you need an 'international draft'.

It can require two signatures from the bank manager, although one usually suffices.

It can be made out for any amount providing you can provide the funds.

The customer's name does not appear on the draft.

The draft is made out to the seller and cannot be transferred.

How do I get a banker's draft?

Any bank can get a banker's draft but it is better to use the bank that has your savings and/or current account.

The customer needs to complete a written application form.

There is a fee, which will be found in your bank's tariffs and charges. These vary depending on the bank, but start at around £12.

The bank will issue the draft after checking that the customer has the necessary funds available.

The draft cannot be amended in any way and the bank may insist that it is crossed by adding the words 'account payee not negotiable'.

What happens if the banker's draft is lost?

If the draft should go missing in the post you can take steps to re-coup the money.

Contact the bank that issued the draft and explain what has happened.

Your bank will then contact the international bank in the country where the draft was sent. It can then confirm whether the draft has been cashed.

If the draft has not been cashed the bank can issue a refund or replacement draft up to six years after the draft has been originally drawn.

The bank may require some additional proof of attempted purchase.

> *Top tip:* Remember, if the draft is cashed but no item was received the problem needs to be resolved with the seller; the bank is not liable.

ELECTRONIC MONEY TRANSFER

A more secure way of sending high-value transactions is through electronic transfer.

What is electronic transfer?

Similar to a banker's draft but more secure, as the bank deals with transferring the money rather than relying on the postal service.

In the UK there is the CHAPS system which is a same-day money transfer system between UK banks.

Check with your bank the cut-off point for the day's transfer and the cost.

For sending money abroad you can use International Payments. This can take either 2–3 days with an 'express transfer' or 5–7 working days via normal transfer.

There is a tracking service for both UK and International so you are able to trace exactly where your money is.

The advantage to the seller with this system is that there is no fee to pay at their end.

The disadvantage is that the seller needs to provide you with their bank account number and sort code, and they may not wish to do this.

What do I do?

First, you need to obtain the seller's bank details.

Ask your bank about the service and charges.

Fill out a form.

The bank does the rest.

You can log onto www.bba.org.uk and search for information on 'Banker's Drafts' and 'Electronic Transfers'.

SWITCH

Most people with bank accounts have Switch or Maestro cards, which allow them to submit their card and see the money withdrawn immediately. It's a guaranteed payment method because if you don't have the money in your bank account or exceed an approved overdraft the Switch card is rejected when the seller tries to use it. Nevertheless, it's not unknown for such cards to be cloned or replicated in some form, so do exercise caution. Switch offers:

 A minimal charge to the seller for receiving the money, particularly compared to the charges for accepting credit cards.

 An automated payment that avoids the need to write and send cheques or any other form of cash.

 No cost to the buyer.

> **Top tip:** Obtain the seller's phone number and postal address before making payment in case of any discrepancies.

What if something goes wrong?

 Print out your order and the details of the seller's terms and conditions.

 Raise concerns with the seller first to try and resolve the matter.

 Contact your bank and ask them to sort out the problem with their charge-back policies.

For further information on Switch/Maestro visit www.switch.
co.uk or www.cardwatch.org.uk who have information on
'Staying Safe Online' and 'Tips 4 Internet Shopping'.

CREDIT CARDS

These cost the seller money to process and not every seller will
have a business account through which they have the means to
accept credit cards in the first place. Just to hire a credit-card
machine for a seller can cost £25+ a month in rental and a
2.5% charge on each transaction processed. So:

If the seller accepts Switch, postal orders or credit cards
see, before bidding, if a deal can be done on something such as
postage if you pay by the alternative methods, which are clearly
cheaper for the seller. There is no harm in asking.

Remember the usual term is 48–54 days interest free on a
credit card, after which interest is charged and if you already
have a considerable credit-card balance, buying on eBay via
credit card will increase this balance all the time and therefore
increase the interest you are paying.

Shop around for the best and cheapest 0% interest deals
on credit cards rather than pay interest, which can in some
cases come to 30%.

Review the credit card you are using every month for a
better deal.

Consider an online credit card with a company such as
Egg, where you can transfer funds electronically from your
bank account across to the Egg account and thus manage your

overall finances and eBay money more efficiently online.

Feel free to use a credit card if there is a special offer running which means the more you use it the more points you get for further spending or the more cash-back credit you receive.

Most credit cards offer automatic insurance cover should an item arrive broken, damaged or not as described but check your card issuer's individual terms and conditions to see whether this is the case, how it works and what level of cover is offered.

Top tip: If you are struggling to meet credit-card payments already don't use a credit card for any eBay purchases. You shouldn't be buying anything on eBay until you have settled your credit-card bills as there is no such thing as a bargain when you are paying monthly interest on a credit card.

Sorry – Item Not Won

This means just that. If you fail to win the item that you were interested in then you will again receive an email telling you so. eBay keeps you informed by emails all the way through the auction; if you are outbid then you receive an email. If you haven't won then don't be disheartened; just keep trying as nine times out of ten you will find the item again, even cheaper than before, and bag yourself a bargain. eBay may also offer you alternative auctions for similar or identical pieces. However, if the email indicates that the reserve has not been met, rather than that the item has been successfully bid for by someone else, it may be worth emailing the seller asking if the item will be re-listed at a later date and at a lower reserve. It is also possible that the seller may be prepared to do a deal with you even though your bid did not succeed this time round. eBay does have strict rules on 'behind the scenes' deals so make sure you follow the eBay etiquette.

Top tip: Reilly Carver went for it with her first eBay buy, 'I saw a £3,000 dining table and chairs listed and at this money it was a rather brave and very scary first-time buy. I was moving to an old house and needed a new dining table so I typed 'dining table' into the search engine and up came this amazing table and twelve chairs. It's handmade from three pieces of oak sitting with metal legs and twelve metal chairs. It was listed with a starting bid of £2,000 but had a reserve. I was the sole bidder with £2,500 but then the auction deadline passed. As my bid was below the reserve it went unsold but the vendor listed it again and this time I went straight to £3,000 and won it. I had contacted the seller and asked to go to see it and she said yes, but I didn't manage to get to Sussex and took the risk of bidding because she sounded very genuine. It was a fantastic buy and looks amazing in my dining room. I took a gamble but it paid off and I loved the whole eBay experience. It was a great adrenaline rush bidding at the end and waiting to see if I had won.'

SECOND-CHANCE OFFER

Sellers can offer the under-bidder a chance to purchase the item if the transaction between themselves and the winning bidder falls through. Please note that this offer will come via eBay and appears on your 'My eBay' page.

Top tip: Accept a second-chance offer only if it comes from the seller, via the eBay system. Any transaction not using the 'Place Bid' or 'Buy It Now' buttons is considered an off-site transaction. Fraudsters are impersonating eBay sellers and emailing the under-bidder direct, offering them the item. The buyer then sends the money and does not receive the goods because they were never available. The fraudster banks the money and there is no come-back because it was not an official eBay transaction.

WHAT CAN GO WRONG?

Most reputable sellers will give you a full refund on return of the item once it has been agreed that the item does not fit or match the description. Remember, however, that they do not have to refund your money simply because you have changed your mind and if the seller can prove that the item was delivered even though you claim it was not, you need to prove how and why it never arrived. Do not jump to leave negative feedback as this only goes against you and will probably ensure that you receive negative feedback back from the seller. Most problems can be sorted out as long as you both work together and are patient. Remember, the most common problems are:

The item is not as described in the original listing. You need to contact the seller and try to resolve your problems, but take care to make it quite clear why the item is not fulfilling the promise made on the seller's description. You cannot reject a broken item if the seller made it quite clear the item was broken in the first place. However, if the seller had said it was broken in one place and it arrives broken in several places then you would have the right to contest the transaction.

The item is damaged. You should have your insurance to fall back on. Make sure you notify the seller of the problem so that he or she can ensure the ball starts to roll when you make a claim, and never throw the item away. In the case of the Post Office insurance, the Post Office may well wish to see the damaged item to assess whether it has been broken by the Post Office in delivery or was not properly packaged in the first place. I once took delivery of an Arts and Crafts stained-glass casement window that had been wrapped in cereal boxes and bubble wrap and brown tape – needless to say the rattling made it clear to me that the glass had smashed. Obviously, glass requires great care and a hard outer box for posting. The Post Office sent down an inspector months later to see the damaged item and the packaging it had arrived in.

The item disappears and never arrives. You need to remain in touch with the seller, who should, depending which Post Office service they used, be able to track the item during its transport from the seller's home to yours. Delays, particularly around Christmas, are inevitable so be patient and if the item still does not turn up a report needs to be filed with the Post Office so a claim can be made. In most cases, sellers will simply accept this loss and refund the money, but if you are experiencing problems with the seller you can turn to eBay for help by accessing the help pages on the eBay home page.

The item arrives with duty to be paid. This is not something that will happen within the UK site as all our duty is domestic and paid for within the purchase price unless stated as an additional cost, for example £100 plus VAT @ 17.5% = £117.50. However, buying from non-EU countries means import duty needs to be paid on purchases over and above £18. The charges vary depending on the purchase price of the item. Obviously, some people take a chance and attempt to get American sellers to declare on the front of the package that the item is 'a gift' but the 'gift' allowance is £36 so it can still be liable for duty. Duty is not something that is optional, however; it is a charge that is enforced by law and should always be paid and the value of an item declared truthfully. For further information contact HM Customs and Excise's National Helpline Services on 0845 010 9000 or visit www.hmce.gov.uk.

You don't like the item. Tough! You bid on it, you bought it and just because you don't like it now that's no reason to expect the seller to refund your money. However, there are some sellers who do offer a no-questions-asked returns policy – but you need to check this and reach agreement with the seller before you bid.

eBay can intervene. If something goes wrong and you do not get the response you want from the seller then you can go to the 'Square Deal Online Dispute Resolution' link and file a case to be considered by an independent adjudicator. It's a free service and filing the case should take no more than five minutes.

Fakes, forgeries, counterfeit. eBay has strict and tough policies on those selling fake designer goods, forged signatures and counterfeit videos and other items. You can click on the link from the eBay home page to see the items that eBay will not allow to be sold but remember it's still 'buyer beware'. There are some clever wordings that can catch people out, e.g. 'Burberry-like/type/style/look' and 'authentic antique reproduction'.

Top tip: Having paid the equivalent of £300 for a much-sought-after original 1950s beehive handbag that I had wanted and saved for over an eight-year period, I was horrified when it arrived all the way from the States to my door with a bill for £90 import duty. If you refuse to pay the duty the item will be returned to the seller and as it is the buyer's responsibility to know that duty is due and needs to be paid the seller could opt to leave you bad feedback. So my beehive handbag cost me £390! Should this happen to you, remember to get a copy of the duty receipt from the delivery service, whether this is the Post Office, Parcel Force, or any other service, as it's your only proof that the duty has been paid.

Done Deal – Feedback Time

Once you have successfully or unsuccessfully completed an eBay transaction you will need to leave a feedback comment. This is a simple system of comments and rating that eBay users leave for each other in order for other users to identify whether they are dealing with a reputable user or not. You can do this in one of two ways. Either click the 'feedback forum' icon at the bottom of the home page > Leave Feedback > Sign In. This will then list every transaction that needs feedback left. Alternatively, click into 'My eBay' on the home page > Items Sold/Won > Leave Feedback. This icon is found next to each item that you have either bought or sold.

POSITIVE FEEDBACK

A positive feedback left increases a seller's or buyer's rating by +1.

Feedback assures other sellers that you are a reputable and reliable eBayer.

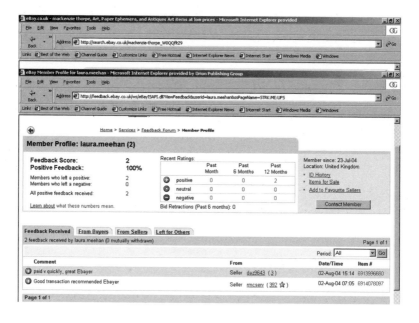

eBay user feedback profile.

What should I write?

Excellent seller, highly recommended to other eBay users.

A credit to eBay, definitely trade with again.

 Perfect transaction, a pleasure to deal with.

NEGATIVE FEEDBACK

 A negative feedback results in a seller's or buyer's rating going down by 1.

 This is shown in the feedback rating box and allows other eBayers to see how many negatives have been registered.

Try to resolve the issues before leaving negative or neutral feedback. Do not rush into feedback and only leave negative or neutral as a last resort, for instance:

 If you have paid for the item but it never arrived and the eBay user is refusing to make contact with you to resolve the problem and refund your money.

 If you have sold an item, received payment, sent it out but the payment by cheque bounced and the buyer is not responding to your emails to send payment again.

NEUTRAL FEEDBACK

Neutral feedback is usually left when a transaction does not run as smoothly as expected but does not warrant leaving negative feedback.

 A neutral feedback equates to 0 so does not affect the eBayer's score but does show up in the eBay user's feedback rating box.

Neutral feedback also gives you an opportunity to leave a comment that others can read but I really do not see the point of leaving this if you have received the item and it is as described.

What should I leave as a negative or neutral comment?

It is entirely up to you what you write but steer clear of abuse, foul language or slanderous remarks. Whatever you decide to write is public so make sure that it is a fair comment and the facts are correct. Keep it simple:

Goods not arrived, ignored emails, buyer beware not reliable eBayer.

Failed to pay for item, not serious about eBay, sellers be careful.

Service was good but could have been better as the item took three weeks to arrive.

If feedback is left that you want to reply to this is simply done through the feedback forum. Click onto Homepage > Feedback forum > Reply to Feedback Received. You can reply with your comments and explain why a transaction didn't run smoothly, etc.

Blocking a Bidder

A seller has the right not to sell to an eBayer and can block them from bidding. Also, if a bid has already been placed this can be removed. A seller will block if they feel you have too much negative feedback or if you live in a country that they do not sell to. You can ask to be unblocked by contacting the seller through their listing page and trying to establish and resolve any issues that they might have with you.

> *Top tip:* Gary Waring, eBay trader, whose business turns over £1.5m a year on eBay, has this advice for new eBay buyers leaving feedback: 'New eBayers are a devil for leaving negative, some do not even contact the seller when there is a problem and just go ahead and leave the negative or neutral. It takes time to sort out the various winning items, especially when you are listing at the rate that Abbey Antiques are and new eBayers do not take into account that an item will not be with them within twenty-four hours of the auction finishing.'

ebay.com

If you feel that you are brave enough to bid on something from overseas you do not necessarily have to log onto this site but on the home page there is a box on which you click for 'items available to the UK'. This will list everyone willing to post overseas to the UK as well as residents within – and not every eBay seller is prepared to send outside their own country. But remember:

Some will say 'ship worldwide', others 'ship worldwide, excluding Europe' – be careful to bid only on items where the seller is prepared to send to you. Bidding on an item that falls outside the seller's postal category can mess up that seller's auction. However, I have also found that many, even if they do not post to the UK, will consider doing this if your bid is successful, your buyer's rating is high and you are prepared to accept the additional transport costs.

There's certainly an argument that you are more likely to get yourself a bargain from the States, particularly when the pound is strong against the dollar. At the moment, my husband is busy buying Ralph Lauren polo shirts for golf from ebay.com at the equivalent of £10 a time rather than £50 a time from House of Fraser and they are genuine Ralph Lauren, not fakes or counterfeit. The time taken to complete a transaction overseas is longer simply because of transportation issues but there's no reason, providing both sides understand the geographical restrictions, why a sale should not take place and proceed perfectly. After all, millions of cross-continent eBay sales take place every day without a problem.

Currency variations will take place and sellers may list a set currency exchange rate that they are prepared to accept regardless of the actual bank-listed exchange rate – if you bid on an auction that details a set currency rate in the listing you have to accept this.

Transferring money to an international seller may be more expensive, as some credit-card companies charge higher fees for international transactions and certainly international money orders are prohibitively expensive to buy from UK banks for anything other than the absolute bargain of the year. Make sure you check out the payment terms and assess the cost of these before bidding.

PayPal is accepted by most international eBay sellers and using this can help speed up a transaction.

 Be realistic about the time it will take to receive an item, as airmail to and from the States is far quicker than by sea, which can mean the item is only guaranteed to arrive within three months!

 Bear in mind the geography of the seller's country, as many American sellers live hundreds of miles from their local bank, Post Office or shipping service and may only make a trip into town to pick up payments or send out items once a week or a fortnight.

 Extra packaging charges may be levied by the seller who will wish to make sure that the item is doubly well wrapped for such a long voyage.

 Check out import duty.

Top tip: Look at items abroad, especially America, at strange times of the day, such as first thing in the morning as this is when the American residents are asleep and you could win something a lot cheaper because there are not as many bidders around. It's also worth checking out international time zones and international and individual country's bank holidays as once again these tend to be quieter times within that country's geographical area and can mean less competition. So, for example, on American Independence Day on 4 July the nation is busy celebrating, as it is again on Thanksgiving Day on 24 November – arguably good times to buy from Americans. Similarly, many UK buyers argue that August is a good time to buy because so many other potential bidders are on holiday. Just bear in mind that lots of seasoned UK sellers also go on holiday because they know that the prices realised for their items will not be as good as at other times in the year and so they refrain from listing items.

Conclusion

- Always be patient with the sellers, particularly if you are buying from another country. It may be the twenty-first century but we have not reached "Beam me up Scottie" technology for item delivery.
- You will find life much easier with a PayPal account but, however you choose to pay, pay promptly. Keep in contact with your seller via email and always alert them to any problems you may have before providing feedback.
- Remember that eBay is your first port of call for customer service, good or bad.
- Never overlook additional postage insurance and possible import charges. These can dramatically increase the overall cost of anything you buy on eBay.
- Don't get carried away – it's very easy to spend money like water, so set yourself a budget and stick to it.

CHAPTER EIGHT

BUILDING AN EBAY BUSINESS

After a lifetime in the antiques and collectables trade in Hereford, Gary Waring finally decided to venture onto eBay. That was back in 1999 and today he is busy running Abbey Antiques, which turns over £1.5m a year. He has spent £500,000 at Bonhams buying stock to sell on eBay and employs some twenty staff. Furthermore, his business is growing. Together with his brother, Richard, Gary visits auction houses all round the country to find items that they feel will sell well on eBay and, contrary to the rest of the auction trade, they tend to specialise in brown furniture. This, to you and me, is the typical oak and mahogany furniture that is often neglected by the traditional antiques trade on the basis that it's out of fashion and hard to sell in today's open market. Clearly, Gary has found a niche, not only when it comes to buying well but also a vehicle through which it sells well, i.e. eBay.

Most of the dealers I speak to at the traditional auction houses insist that items such as 'big brown wardrobes' are only really any good for firewood today. The typical argument is that people's houses are now too small to accommodate such big lumps, that people have too many clothes and prefer fitted wardrobes and that the 'new, retro, modern, minimal' decor styles simply mean that demand for this type of ware has dwindled. I myself have visited and filmed at plenty of auctions where such pieces have struggled to make over £100, which has always seemed a dreadful shame given the quality of the wood and the craftsmanship involved to make such a piece in the first place. Let's face it, it's a testament to the work that these items still exist – I can't imagine an Ikea wardrobe still being in existence in 100 years' time.

Left 1930 limed oak armoire wardrobe/linen press. *Right* 1930 oak drop-leaf barley-twist table.

From humble beginnings Gary's business has grown and he now also runs his own delivery service so that he can ensure each item is delivered directly to the buyer's door. In addition, he has a money-back guarantee so that if a buyer is not happy with the item when it arrives, Abbey Antiques simply issues a full refund and takes the item away again. So it all sounds great, but Gary himself admits, 'I have never worked so hard in all my life. We try to list at least 100 items a week and the hardest part is the follow-up after the auction has finished. This is the most time-consuming, trying to ensure that all the items are packed, emails answered and payment taken.' Gary also insists on making customer care a priority so that the business builds its own database of loyal and regular customers. By listing every item at a starting price of just 1p and with no reserve, Gary estimates at least one in three winning bidders on his items are repeat customers.

Gary adds, 'People love the fact that they can purchase something unusual from the comfort of their own homes and have it delivered to their doorsteps but also it is the fun of the bidding on auction sales. People's adrenaline rushes ensure that something things sell for over the odds, as people get really involved in winning the item. Even though I start everything at 1p, I do obviously make losses – on one in ten items on average. If I have bought something for £200 at auction and only get £50 on eBay, I don't worry too much as that person has had a bargain and so will become a repeat customer and perhaps buy something that gives me profit next time.'

Gary's success is down to plenty of hard graft, testing the market again and again to find what sells and what doesn't and building up his core customer base. This is a business that is coming into its sixth year and, as Gary adds, 'A lot of people start selling on eBay as a hobby and then that hobby turns into a profitable business. But if something does expand then you really have to ensure that you run your business properly. Register for VAT if your turnover is large, which is currently £58,000 or more, register with the Inland Revenue, etc. You will be happy when this is done and if you are making large profits and enough money then it shouldn't be a problem.'

Very few people actually start selling on eBay with the intention of beginning a small business, but many find that, almost by default, within a year or two they are looking at a considerable turnover and one that needs to be treated properly for tax purposes. It's no secret that plenty of people are making money on the side through eBay and treat it almost as if it were a black market when it comes to declaring their earnings to the taxman. However, there's no getting away from taxes and the Inland Revenue has the right to investigate anyone's affairs should it have reason to believe that money is not being declared properly. Tax can then be reclaimed from the individual should a case be proved, and there are crippling interest rates.

Some years ago, the accountant to whom my tax affairs where entrusted disappeared with a substantial amount of money from clients' accounts. Fortunately, I was not among those who actually lost money but what I did lose were all my records and receipts for a three-year period – all of which had been shredded by the accountant before he quite literally 'left the building'. The accountant is currently serving eighteen months, which is about the time it took me and a new, reliable, efficient and trustworthy accountant in the form of Barry Dunning to sort out the mess he left behind. It was a terrible time and really worrying, because I had no idea how the Tax Office or the Inland Revenue would see my predicament. Fortunately, because the case attracted press interest there were plenty of press cuttings proving that I had not been careless, lost or failed to record my financial income and outgoings, but had been subject to the most unfortunate circumstances. Remarkably, and I have to say much to their credit, the Inland Revenue was extremely helpful. Over the period of time, we estimated the income and outgoings to the best of our ability and worked out an overall settlement with the Inland Revenue, which in turn was paid over a period of a few months. It wasn't easy and it was costly in terms of getting professional advice. However, the key lesson was that the Inland Revenue really is there to help and to work with you, not against you, providing you keep in regular contact with them and are completely truthful about your circumstances, income and events. So, if you are one of the ones wondering whether the Inland Revenue is scouring the Internet in search of you, suspecting that you are earning a nice little nest egg from eBay that is not being declared, then you should tackle the issue today – not tomorrow but today. Make contact, make an appointment if necessary, and explain your situation and the Inland Revenue in turn will help you calculate what, if anything, should be paid.

Here's a basic rundown that will keep you out of trouble and help you sleep at night while your auctions are continuing on eBay:

If you are selling unwanted gifts, second-hand items that you yourself previously owned or items that you have bought for one price but end up selling for less than the original retail price you paid, you are probably in the clear as far as declaring tax is concerned.

> *Top tip:* Whatever I buy, other than food, of course, I always ensure that I keep the receipts. In some cases, when I purchase designer clothes in the sales, I actually wear them complete with the original labels tucked inside the collars so that should I decide to sell the items later on eBay they are in as good a condition as possible, thus maximising the potential resale price.

Everyone, no matter how much or how little they sell on eBay, should clarify where they stand with their local Inland Revenue office, which can be located in the *Yellow Pages* or via the local Internet community site for your area.

> *Top tip:* If you are considering turning your eBay business into full-time employment you will probably come under the term 'self-employed' and be charged tax under the 'self-assessment' scheme. Penalties of £100 a time are levied for late payments under self-assessment so it's vital you put at least 25%–40% of your income by to cover the tax that may be due. Any surplus that is not needed can then be reinvested into stock.

National Insurance must also be paid by everyone in work, whether this is working for someone else or a large company or as a self-employed individual. It's not an optional extra and the only people who can get away with not paying it are those who are earning less than the minimum tax threshold. This can be checked at the Inland Revenue office. It can be as little as £8 a month, but again it's something that needs to be paid up front straight away to avoid getting behind with payments and into a financial pickle.

> *Top tip:* As far as the law is concerned you are totally responsible for your own tax matters and ignorance is not a plea when it comes to tackling tax matters. When my former accountant disappeared with £1m+ of pop band *The Verve's* tax money it took two to three years for him to be caught, prosecuted and jailed. However, the band itself still had to pay the tax due to the Inland Revenue, even though the band had, in good faith, already sent this money to the accountant for him to pay it to the taxman.

In order to make a profit you have to have bought something for, let's say, £100 and have sold it for more than that amount, let's say, £150. This is a profit on paper, but you also have the right to deduct from the £50 you have made any costs that you have incurred, within reason, to secure the piece. So, if you had spent £10 on petrol, and a further £17 on commission and charges at the auction to get the piece your profit would be:

£50 - £27, i.e. the expenses of the petrol, commission and charges = £23 profit. It is this £23 that is the actual profit and on which tax will be charged. The amount of tax charged will depend on how much profit you make over the course of an entire tax year, which is somewhat different to a calendar year.

It's vital to keep a record of your transactions throughout. This is one reason why it's important, when selling or buying at boot sales or auctions, to keep either a small exercise book at hand to record your purchases and sales or a dictaphone into which you can verbally record this information before typing it up into the computer later.

> *Top tip:* Don't be tempted to think that you will automatically remember your purchases. Keep all receipts, even if at the time you think they may not be of use. The receipt from an auction purchase is vital to reclaim VAT, as a record for the price paid versus the price you realise for the piece eventually, but so too is the petrol receipt for the petrol you put into the car in order to get to the auction.

Every 5 April is the end of one tax year, with 6 April marking the start of the new tax year. It's important to check with your local Inland Revenue office for any changes to the tax and National Insurance laws that come into effect with the new tax year. Similarly, a good accountant may have some perfectly legal advice on when best to pay yourself some form of income that will make best use of all your personal and company allowances over the two tax years. Only look at such options under professional advice.

> *Top tip:* When you started the business will dictate which date your annual accounting year runs from and your accounting year is completely different to any VAT issues. VAT is charged or repaid every quarter and if you are due to pay VAT one quarter there are heavy penalties for late payment; these are more costly than those levied for late tax payments.

Most computer programs have a basic accounts or expenses sheet layout, which you can manipulate to best suit the type of purchases and sales you are making before saving them to disc as a long-term record of your business, however large or small.

> **Top tip:** In general you need to allow a fifth of all the time you spend on your business for accounting and paperwork purposes. It's great going around buying, selling and, hopefully, making money. The postage and packaging can be a tedious but necessary task – but never underestimate the importance of keeping your records straight. After all, it's your money and it's important that you claim everything you can and make your money work for you.

It's always worthwhile seeking the advice of small business initiatives, including Business Link, in your local area, or similar business forums. For those really planning to make a go of this venture, there are plenty of small business courses run on a part-time and evening school basis from local colleges. These can help you understand your obligations and run your record-keeping more efficiently.

> **Top tip:** Check out the British Bankers' Association website at www.bba.org.uk. There is a section called 'Business Account Finder', which has plenty of information on small businesses and over forty different accounts so that people can decide what is the best way forward for them when setting up a small

business. The *Your Money and the Internet* leaflet is available
through the website, code AEO96 being the most recent one
they have on BBA.

Most high-street banks offer small-business accounts,
which are usually free of charges for the first year or eighteen
months. These have much to recommend them, not least of
which is the fact that this will help you keep your business
transactions, profit, loss and turnover separate from your day-
to-day personal living costs and bank account. Small business
accounts have a threshold and if your business grows to such
an extent that your turnover (the amount of money that you
are taking before any of your running costs, investment in
stock or other expenses are deducted) exceeds this threshold,
your bank manager should consult you about other banking
options.

Top tip: It's the same as any other bargain hunting – you need
to shop around for the best business account that suits you.
Don't be afraid to move your account around and haggle on
the charges you will incur once the 'free' period expires.

Just in case you thought tax was all bad, there are some
tax breaks if you know how to use them. Clock collectors are
cashing in on a tax break that means any profits realised from
the sale of clocks are exempt from capital gains tax. Although
auction houses will never recommend any particular purchase
on the grounds of potential investment, the tax advantage

clearly gives clocks a lead over and above other areas of the collecting market.

> *To tip:* Christie's Clocks and Scientific Instruments expert, Ben Wright, explains, 'Any profit made on the sale of any clock of any age is exempt from capital gains tax. So if you bought a clock for £10,000 and later sold it for £25,000 you do not have to pay capital gains tax on the £15,000 gain. This is a great advantage for those collecting clocks compared to any other area of the collecting market where capital gains tax does apply. We certainly have some collectors who invest in this area purely for the tax break.'

If you are running your business from home you can claim a percentage of your electricity and heating bills, but you will also need to check where you stand in terms of capital gains tax. It is possible that if you later move and sell your property for a profit capital gains tax might apply, which is not the case of course for those selling their main private home not used for business purposes.

> *Top tip:* Everyone's an expert when it comes to tax and making the most of your money, but do not take the advice of anyone other than a professional expert in the field of accountancy or tax. I know of someone who was leaving all their money in a PayPal account and then going to the States every year to transfer it to an American bank account on the basis that the money was staying offshore and therefore making use of the

offshore laws. However, an accountant disputed the legitimacy of this attempt to avoid UK tax, advising that tax would still have been payable on such a transaction – so if in doubt, don't phone a friend, phone a professional.

Insurance

Collecting provides one in three people in this country with hours of pleasure. Whether it's amassing every model or figure in a series or simply enhancing your home's interior with period bits and pieces, before long it's highly likely that your home contents have gone up in value. Whether or not you are a collector, it's standard practice for insurance firms to insist that certain security measures are taken before a home contents policy is valid. If you are using rooms in your home, your shed or your garage for eBay selling stock then it is extremely important you get proper insurance cover; this may be more expensive than domestic insurance because it is for business use. However, any insurance company will require the most basic security measures, which include:

Checking outside doors have deadlocks that conform to British Safety Standards. Some insist on window locks and five-lever mortice locks on the main outer doors too.

Keeping the keys to all locks out of view and away from the locks that they open.

Fitting a burglar alarm. Depending on the value of the home contents policy some insist that the alarm runs through the entire house and is connected to a local police station, while others are satisfied if it covers the main entrance. However, it's important to seek advice from your insurers first before buying one. Many firms insist that the installation of alarms is carried out by companies registered with the National Approval Council for Security Systems.

Keeping a complete list of valuable items along with photographs for identification, serial numbers where applicable and a short description.

Signing up for Neighbourhood Watch schemes. Local police stations provide details and some insurers offer discounts to those who join.

In the Association of British Insurers' free guide called *Beat the Burglar* the advice is simple: 'Mark your property with a property marking kit. Use your postcode and the number of your house. This will help the police to return your property to you. Your local Crime Prevention Office can also offer you advice.' It's a time-consuming job marking each piece this way, but it is worth taking the time to complete the task, as there's nothing worse than becoming the victim of a burglary and then finding that you have no back-up proof of the items taken.

Contents insurance covers the contents of your home against risks including burglary and accidental damage. However, many homeowners fail to update the value of their contents insurance over the years and find out too late that they are nowhere near covered for the true value of stolen items. All insurance policies spell out clearly the risks they cover, and what is not covered. It's vital to read the contents policy document in full, however boring a task this may be. It's what you're not covered for that's most important. Look for clauses that give a maximum ceiling per item stolen. Many insurers expect single items over a certain value to be declared and may then ask for an additional premium in order to cover these goods. Similarly, more than three items in a single category, e.g. books, may be counted by insurers as a collection with extra insurance requirements – even if you don't consider this a collection. If in doubt, call the insurance firm, explain your queries and get a written answer back.

Accidents happen, but if a collectable is damaged it's vital that you complete a report form for the insurers and keep hold of the damaged item. This is your proof of the level of damage. It may be tempting to simply restore the item, but remember that restored pieces are worth less than perfect examples. It may be better to claim and replace the piece, although some insurers may opt to cover the cost of restoration only.

Hiscox is one of the largest insurance firms to specialise in insuring collections. To assess both the risk and the valuation the company needs information on the type of collection. It will make certain assumptions based on the broker who introduced the business to Hiscox, and arrange a house visit if needed. Hiscox's Charles Dupplin, who is responsible for underwriting the high-net-worth insurance policies, explains: 'Most of the Internet auctions tend to be the lower end of the collectable scale at £2,000–£3,000. Few serious collectors would buy something of high value, say £20,000 on a single item, without actually seeing it. Of course, a brand-new client who comes to us with a whole lot of Internet receipts may prove quite difficult and we'd have to verify the collection and the client. There are three basic rules to this type of underwriting: Who's the client?, Who's the client? and Who's the client?'

In terms of premium costs, Hiscox assesses what Charles Dupplin describes as 'a complicated set of internal guidelines covering what the collection is, where it's held, special factors, such as security and storage'. Some top-end collectors even have 24-hour security guards at home to cut the cost of premiums, while others have secure units. However, nothing is totally foolproof. A valuation is a fluid thing, particularly as most collectors' markets have gone up in value over the last three years. It's important to have the valuation reviewed annually if possible but at least every three years.

For insurance purposes it's vital that you check that the insurance firm offering to cover your valuables is either a member of the Association of British Insurers or the British Insurance and Investment Brokers' Association. Both bodies can provide lists of general insurers offering specially tailored insurance schemes for collectables and antiques. Once you have three named insurance companies, get a quote from all of them as it's always advisable to shop around. Cover can vary greatly in cost from one insurer to the next. Remember to:

Provide the insurer with all the information that it requires and do not over-value items or exaggerate what you have. You will only be charged higher cover costs, which if you cannot back up at the time of claim, means you've paid all this for nothing.

Do follow any stipulations made by the insurer for securing valuables. Failure to install the required locks or take precautions by keeping items in cabinets can invalidate a claim.

Review the cover you have every two to three years, or more frequently if you are constantly adding to your collection.

Check whether your household insurer has already got you covered to a certain extent under the general household policy – it may be that this is sufficient and no further insurance cover is necessary.

Connoisseur Policies (see Appendix 2) enables you to purchase units of £5,000 of cover for £25. It is more expensive for ceramics, etc than for comics and postcards, for example. People can log onto the site and get a quote straight away and, if happy, pay for the cover there and then. Follow the simple instructions on the 'buy online' pages on the website and you should be able to buy up to £50,000 of specialist insurance cover within a matter of minutes. Premiums start at £25 per year.

Top tip: **Cover your less valuable items (up to £500 maximum per item) as collectables and then buy specific units under the relevant headings for your more valuable items and collections. Premiums vary according to the type of item insured and pictures and furniture, for example, cost less to insure than brittle articles, clocks or coins.**

CONCLUSION

I am in a hotel in Bromsgrove, Worcestershire, checking in the afternoon before a *Car Booty* rummage and with just a few hours to spare to write the conclusion to this book which has been seventeen years in the making. So I plug myself into my U2 Special Edition iPod (which I'm convinced will be a collectable of the future) and take off for a walk. Passing a cottage hospital, I spot a skip laden with potentially recyclable goodies: doors, carpet remnants and what looks like a pair of mahogany legs sticking out. After checking with a bemused receptionist, I enlist the help of the chef to extract the chair from the skip. It turns out to be a very respectable, green toile upholstered, pretty bedroom chair, but unfortunately the rain has already done its worst and the upholstery is utterly soaked. A great shame, as I have no doubt it could have made at least £15–£20 at a car boot sale and possibly more on eBay. So today was not the day for a great skip find but it proves the point that you must always be on the lookout and never too proud to poke about in the search for a bargain and a profit.

In fact, my conclusion is that there is no 'conclusion'; it's simply impossible to switch off. Your eyes are always open, scanning everything around you 24/7 for a potential profitable sale. How much profit is almost irrelevant; it's the thrill of the chase, the fun of the find and the satisfaction of the sale. The more you try, the more you learn and there's a market for just about everything, whether it's nostalgia that drives buyers to part with their money as they purchase a long-lost childhood toy or a mum searching for cheap but good clothes for her children.

Nostalgia certainly drives the collectables market and even manufacturers are cashing in. Take Hornby, the model railway company. It recently announced its sales figures for last year were £39m and it expects to increase its annual sales by a further £5.6m on that figure this year, thanks to 'older male collectors buying train sets'. Then there's the Japanese toy company, Tomy, which has launched a limited edition of 3,000 'Piggy Cook' toys costing £74.99 each. This particular toy was first launched in 1965 and is the first of an entire range of reproductions the company hopes will boost its sales and its profits. Last week I managed to buy the original version for just £48, safe in the knowledge that an original will, at the very least, keep its value and, thanks to the publicity generated from the new launch of the reproduction, may increase in value. Time has proved that an original 1965 will always outstrip a reproduction. Raleigh, the bicycle company, recently recognised that nostalgia-buying may be sustainable. It re-launched its classic 1970s 'Chopper' last year at a retail price of £199.99 and in November last year added a re-launched version of the 'Tomahawk' bike costing £99.99. Raleigh managing director, Mark Gouldthorp, admits that the Nottingham-based company owes at least 8% of its increased sales to this range alone, which he also agrees is driven purely by nostalgia. Those in their thirties and forties are buying these

The original 1965 Piggy Cook cost £48, while the 2005 reproduction is priced at £74.99.

bikes if not for themselves then for their offspring to enjoy. Clearly, few remember flying over the handlebars and suffering grazed knees and split lips. Originally launched in 1971, the Chopper Mark I had to be withdrawn because of safety standards, but in time for Christmas 1971 the Chopper Mark II was launched, followed by the special collectors' Silver Jubilee Chopper in 1977. Today this can realise £1,270 on eBay.

As a baby boomer I am one of the 50% of people living today who were born between 1946 and 1965, but the population is dwindling, and the younger generation rarely wants to inherit our collections of clutter – hence the *Car Booty* clear-outs. Within the next ten years or so many baby boomers will be downsizing – cashing in on their property values to fund their pensions. It's just possible we could see a flood of clearance over the next twenty years that outstrips the demand created by an ever-shrinking and somewhat disinterested younger generation. If this happens, prices could plummet and cashing in collections might at best return no more than the original sum invested.

The next few years will see the market split into those specialising in selling or buying nostalgic items and those who are simply recycling their household items for cash. There will be people, such as Jo Wilshaw, who falls into both categories. A mother of a four-year-old, Jo, thirty-five, sold her son's first bed on eBay once he had outgrown it. It made £40 – £10 more than she paid for it three years earlier. Jo explains, 'I have sold lots of my son's clothes and old videos on eBay and find it really useful. In fact, I am now starting to go to proper local auctions and take a chance buying the odd box of mixed, cheap lots and then splitting them all up and selling each item individually on eBay. Overall, I am finding that I make a good profit on each box, even if individual items sometimes don't sell for a lot. It's something I can do for me and me alone.'

But she's not alone. In fact, she's one of a growing population of all ages who are taking to eBay to make money. Georgina Newman from Surrey, for example, started buying children's clothes from eBay just a year ago for her three children aged six, seven and just fourteen months. A year later, she is now fitting in her role as mum with her own self-employed business selling children's clothing on eBay. She sources this from a British wholesaler. Georgina explains, 'I usually list everything on 'Buy It Now'. My best sale was a pair of boy's trousers which usually only retail for around £6 but actually sold for £21.' Not everything sells, and Georgina admits that this, and finding the time around the children, are the downsides of her new career. However, she adds, 'I am now getting repeat customers because I have proved myself reliable by sending out everything the following day through first-class post. There's no doubt that eBay has given me an opportunity to still work despite the children and without the site I wouldn't be able to earn a living at all.'

Resourcefulness and an ability to learn and adapt to the market are the two main skills required to become a successful boot sale buyer and eBay seller, although many would have you believe otherwise. And a bit of lateral thinking never goes amiss. On 8 January 2005, I read an article in a national newspaper about the *Beano* having to pulp its entire weekly issue and immediately realised that there was a potential collectable here. It seems that the comic was going to print with a new ball-boy character called Henry Thierry when the publishers DC Thomson got cold feet, worried that it might offend Thierry Henry and the Arsenal football team. Out went the order to pulp the 200,000 copies and replace it with another ball-boy story. *Beano* editor Ewan Kerr told me, 'It's the first time in sixty-six years that the children's comic has been pulped, although some issues did manage to get into circulation as advertisers were sent a courtesy copy, although how many are on the open market is uncertain.' Interestingly, Mr Kerr would neither confirm nor deny whether or not he had himself secured one of the 'pulped' copies. The *Beano* Number 1, first issued on 30 July 1938, sold for £6,800 in 1999 at Comic Book Postal Auctions. Three years later the same auction house sold an identical example, which realised £7,500, then last year a third identical example realised a whopping £12,100. Given the way that the price paid for the Number 1 has increased it's clear that demand for *Beano*s is not likely to abate in the near future. The natural assumption can only be that there are plenty of *Beano* collectors who would pay good money to get hold of one of the 200,000 'pulped' 8 January issues. The *Beano* Number 1 cost twopence when first issued and there are fewer than twelve copies thought to exist today. With very few of the 200,000 8 January 2005 issues known to have survived, the odds are favourable that this will indeed be valuable, not only in years to come, but immediately if anyone who owns a copy can find a buyer who wants a copy. Despite my best efforts to date, I have not been able to find one, although I wouldn't mind betting that before the year is out one pops up on eBay.

It's all about lateral thinking – something Buckingham Palace was clearly lacking when it allowed detectives to return the controversial 'fancy dress' outfit, featuring a Nazi swastika and worn by Prince Harry, to a shop in Cirencester. The furore surrounding the appearance of Prince Harry in such a tactless, tasteless and arguably offensive outfit, was fuelled by the photographs flashed around the world. As a result, the outfit has become notorious. The owner of the shop has now taken it off hire, but no doubt has stored it away for the future. It's an unfortunate fact of life that within the militaria market, Nazi and SS memorabilia has a huge collectability and following. I have chosen not to cover the topic in its wider sense. To do so would be impossible without mentioning the area that for the last six to eight years has boomed – the Nazi militaria market. To build a collection of such items, which represent some of the most horrendous actions against the Jewish culture and which many of our families fought against, would seem to me to be unjustifiable. To write about it would simply help promote it more. However, on this occasion, it is worth noting that carelessness can cost reputations if not lives. I would not be at all surprised if, in years to come, this most notorious of 'fancy dress' outfits surfaces on eBay. Indeed, my own investigations to date among dealers and auctioneers who have some idea of its potential value would estimate its value at around £50,000–£80,000 at least. We can only hope, of course, that should it ever resurface and be sold the money will at the very least go to charity or that eBay itself will have no part in the sale. I suspect that the lady who currently owns the outfit will have had more than a dozen approaches from individuals seeking to buy it with a view to making a profit.

Instinct plays a part in this too. I'm utterly addicted to the 1990s *Lovejoy* series. I've bought the series on DVD from eBay for between £5 and £10 under the £40 price they retail for. The programme revolves around roguish antiques dealer Lovejoy and his 'divvy' moments. It seems a 'divvy' is someone who can go to a boot sale, auction or fair and immediately has a gut instinct there is something in the room which no one else has spotted is a hidden gem. While writing this book I was contacted by a 'divvy' who had purchased an oil painting at a boot sale for £1 and sold it at auction for £6,800. Being a journalist by trade is the nearest I have ever come to being a 'divvy'. Just as estate agents say 'location, location, location' a journalist mantra is 'check the facts, check the facts and then check them again'. This I did, only to discover the auction house has no record of any painting selling for £6,800 let alone one purchased at a boot sale for £1. However, in 2003 Sotheby's did sell a job lot of nineteen items for £750 in its sale of the contents of Fulbeck Hall in Lincolnshire. Just six months later Bonhams sold a rare seventeenth-century cameo of Shah Jahan for £520,000. What's the connection? Well, the half-a-million-pound cameo came from the £750 box of nineteen items. Such is the myth and magic of the world of boot sales, bargain buys and eBay sales.

For the rest of us, take heart and take a chance. Think about the gentleman we filmed for *Car Booty*, who made £800 at a boot sale dealing his father's antiques and £600 on eBay. His father's set of three Guinness Carlton ware toucans presented to him when he was a pub landlord brought in £350, while a rare Wade moneybox issued in a limited edition of 1,000 in 1992 to promote the film *Fried Green Tomatoes at the Whistlestop Café* made £280. Not only had the moneybox been a free promotional gift at the time, but the gentleman had retrieved it from a skip following an office clear-out only a year before. He was shocked by the price it made but not as shocked as I was by his next comment: 'Actually, there was a box of them and I've still got the other nine.' It's what makes boot sales and eBay such great fun and so addictive – the myth of the

£1 painting sold for £6,800 and the magic of the skip find of Wade moneyboxes worth £2,800. According to a survey by NatWest, we have an estimated £3.5bn worth of clutter in our homes, so just remember, no matter what, come rain or shine there's always a boot sale bargain out there – even if it is in the skip at the end of the sale.

Just in case you were wondering about my most expensive buy – it was the Clarice Cliff charger in the 'Latona Dahlia' pattern mentioned earlier, which was purchased at a boot sale for £1 and I bought at Christie's for £1,976!

APPENDIX I: BOOT SALES

The following boot sales are the ones at which I have filmed and I recommend them to all keen boot-salers.

BERKSHIRE
Ascot Racecourse Car Parks
High Street
Ascot
Berkshire
Tel: 01344 291133
Bought fabulous 1950s dress here for £5. I can't get into it but it's lovely anyway.

Taplow Car Boot
Main A4, Bath Road
Opposite Taplow Station
Maidenhead
Berkshire
Tel: 07956 486448
www.giantcarboot.co.uk
Held every Sunday afternoon except Bank Holidays when it is held on the Monday. 1 p.m. until 5 p.m.

BRISTOL
Bristol (covered boot sale)
Tollgate Car Park
Dale Street
Bristol
BS2 9DA
Tel: 01179 222 198
A very windy, cold and quite depressing location on a multi-storey car park, but packed on every level.

BUCKINGHAMSHIRE
Denham Car Boot (Saturdays)
Main A40, Denham Roundabout
Junction 1 off M40
Near Uxbridge
Buckinghamshire
www.giantcarboot.co.uk
This was a goldmine for a Border Fine Arts piece in 2004. The only problem is the lack of toilets. Also bought a Metropolitan Museum of Art David Hockney poster from his retrospective exhibition in 1988. It cost £3 and is valued at £150–£200.

Milton Keynes National Bowl
Milton Keynes
MK4 1GA
More market than boot sale but a good mix of dealers and general public stallholders.

West Wycombe Boot Sale
Cowleaze Field
A40
West Wycombe
Buckinghamshire
Tel: 01981 250591
Colin Melbourne vases £5 each at the end of the day, and worth £100 on eBay. Also great venue with real genuine boot-salers.

CUMBRIA
Penrith Boot Sale
Skirsgill
Penrith

Cumbria
CA11 0DN

DORSET
Wimbourne Road
Poole
Dorset
Bought some good
Police 1980s coloured
picture discs here for
£10 the lot – great
Retro stuff.

Left These blue vinyl
records cost £10 for
the lot.

Ringwood Boot Sale
Ashleyheath
Horton Road
Dorset

ESSEX
Asda Boot Sale
North Shoebury Road
(Next to Asda)
Shoeburyness
Essex
Tel: 07785 564855
This is a great boot sale for anything
and everything. I bought a set of fan-
tastic glass-topped 1960s nest of
tables for just £6.

Barleylands
Barleylands Road
Billericay
Essex
A129
Website: www.barleylands.co.uk
Great for kids in the summer as it
has bouncy castles and plenty of ice

cream stalls. About 50:50 market
and boot sale.

Bonzers Boot sale (Thursdays)
Romford
A127
Essex
Huntley and Palmer tin purchased
here for 50p that was made in just
one year, 1899–1900 and is worth
£100–£150. Also purchased some
fabulous William Morris print curtains for £2. Fabulous mid-week
boot sale for those who can't wait
until Sunday.

This tin was only produced for one
year in 1899–1900. I bought it at a
boot sale for 50p it is worth
£100–£150.

Chelmsford County Showground
Great Leighs
Essex
CM3 1QP
A good mix of stalls of genuine boot-
salers. Great for nearly-new toys.

Chigwell Car Boot Sale
Chigwell Rise (next to David Lloyds)
Essex
Tel: 01279 871117
Fabulous genuine designer clothes
here, including Burberry man's
jumper and Katherine Hamnett
jumper for £10 each. Also bought a
great Marcel Breuer leather chair for
£15 that would cost £250 to buy
brand new – it's a design classic.

Dunton Boot Sale
Dunton Road
Off A127
Near Basildon
Essex
Tel: 01277 624979
I kitted out my son with clothes,
toys, a buggy, desks, brand-new
curtains and loads more from this
one. Quite a mix, including more
'market-type' stalls and good for
plants and garden stuff too.

Epping
North Weald Airfield
Essex
McFarlane tin shaped as an anvil
cost a whacking £60 but sold for
£280 on eBay.

Lazybones Boot Sale
Whitehouse Farm
A130
Rettendon
Essex
Bought a whole box of Brittain's zoo
animals for £4. They are arguably
worth £100+.

Stevenson's Farm
Southend Arterial Road (A127)
Nevendon
Basildon
Essex
SS14 3JH
Great for designer clothes,
collectables and toys. Gets packed
and definitely one of the largest in
the summer. Brilliantly run and still
my favourite. Dean's bear and Art
Deco cigarette box for £20. I also
know someone who bought a
Moorcroft 'Anemone' bowl for 50p
that was later valued at £300.

GREATER MANCHESTER
Indoor/Outdoor Car Boot
295 Talbot Road
Stretford
Manchester

HAMPSHIRE
Bordon Boot Sale
Osborne Farm
Bordon
Hampshire
GU35 9LW
Great, great venue, as the Farm Shop
has a fabulous restaurant serving
proper fried breakfasts. Bought a
great bar stool for £20 shaped as a
pint of Guinness. The stallholders
are very friendly too.

HERTFORDSHIRE
Cuffley
Cattlegate Road
Nr Potters Bar
Herts.
Purchased great snakeskin handbag
complete with purse and mirror for
£12 which later made £120 on eBay.

St Albans
Herts. Showground
Redbourn
Herts.

IRELAND
Bangor Rugby Club
Bloomfield Road South
Bangor
Tel: Harry on 028 91458182
Held every Sunday at the rugby club.

Fairyhouse Racecourse (market and
car boot)
Ratoath
Co. Meath
www.fairyhouseracecourse.ie

KENT
Sandwich Drews Field
Kent
Tel: 01304 829822
Victorian fireplace found abandoned
and reclaimed.

LANCASHIRE
Clitheroe (indoor and outdoor)
Auction Mart
Ribblesdale Centre
Lincoln Way
Clitheroe
Lancashire
BB7 1QD
Good all year round and a good mix
of items and stalls, all well priced.
Good for board games such as Spit-
ting Image, On the Buses and
Colditz that can make £20+ on eBay.

A blast from the past.

Accrington Market
Peel Street
Accrington
Lancashire

Whyndyke Farms
Junction 4 M55
Blackpool
Lancashire

Tommyfield Market Car Boot Sale
Albion Street
Oldham
Lancashire

LEICESTERSHIRE
Melton Mowbray
The Cattle Market
Leicestershire
This is huge and run very efficiently
with plenty of good food stalls and
decent toilets. I bought a Wedgwood
'Thomas the Tank Engine' beaker
for 50p and a Barbola mirror for £1
which made £60 on eBay.

Bath Lane
Moira
Junction 11 M42
Leicester
Tel: 01283 548024

LONDON
Wimbledon Stadium
Plough Lane
Wimbledon
London
SW17 0BL
Bought a great 1920s kitchen dresser
base here for £7. Renovated by
Mark Franks, it's now worth £400.

MIDLANDS
Hard-standing Car Boot Sale
Mercia Leisure Park
Lockhurst Lane
Coventry

Balsall Common RFC
Meer End (A4177)
West Midlands

Arrow Car Boot Sale
Bartleet Road
Washford
Redditch
B98 0GB

Hams Lane
Hams Hill
Nr Coleshill
Birmingham
B46 1AW

NOTTINGHAMSHIRE
Oldcotes Boot Sale
Situated on the A634 Oldcotes to
Blyth Road
Near to the A1 roundabout at Blyth
Worksop
Nottinghamshire
(opposite garden
centre)
S81 8JE
**Bought 56 Butlins
badges for £60. One
from 1954 realised
£58 on eBay.**

Sherwood Forest
Farm Park
Edwinstowe
Nottinghamshire
Tel: 01623 629219

**My bargain Butlins
badges, picked up
at a Nottingham car
boot sale.**

SCOTLAND
Blochairn Fruit Farm
Blochairn Road
Glasgow
**Known as Scotland's largest car boot
sale; held every Sunday.**

SOMERSET
Yeovil Showground
A37 Dorchester Road
Yeovil
Somerset
Tel: 07979 345914

Bought some great picture discs and
Swatch watches here and a Carlton
ware Denim teapot for £5 which
sold for £25 on ebay.com

SURREY
Nuthill Fruit Farm
London Road
Guildford
Surrey
GU23 7LW
Bought great Merrythought tortoise
here for 50p, a
fabulous set of
garden chairs
for £5 and a
framed piece of
the Berlin Wall.

**A genuine piece
of the Berlin
Wall and barbed
wire.**

SUSSEX
Brighton South Central Station
Queens Road
Brighton
BN1 3XP
More a true outdoor antiques mar-
ket with real dealers than a boot sale
– worth going just to spot Fatboy
Slim. Bought a Bullseye Bully from
the TV show for 50p which made
£58 on eBay. Hardstanding.

Ford
Airfield
Nr Arundel
Sussex
Hard-standing – great location, very
friendly and gets very packed.

TYNESIDE

Afternoon Car Boot
Seaham Coast Road
Tyneside
Tel: 01429 835929

WALES

Abergavenny Flea Market
Market Street
www.abergavennymarket.co.uk
Flea market held every Wednesday.

Carew Airfield CC Site
Sageston
Tenby
Pembrokeshire
South Wales
SA70 8SH
**Held on Sundays in one of the
hangars, it is a very large market and
equally large car boot sale.**
Singleton Hospital
Staff Car Park
Sketty Lane
Sketty
Swansea
SA2 8QA
Tel: 01792 285331

Held every Saturday all year round
except for three weeks over Christmas and New Year.

YORKSHIRE

Car Boot Sale
Broad Street Car Park
Halifax
Tel: 01422 359034

Car Boot Fair
Thirsk Racecourse
Ripon Road
A61
Yorkshire

Ripon Racecourse
Afternoon Car Boot
Yorkshire

For more details on your local
boot sale you can find all the
information that you need in the
publication *The Car Boot & Fairs
Calendar*. For more information
on this publication please visit
www.carbootcalendar.com or email
detailscarboot@aol.com.

APPENDIX 2:
USEFUL CONTACTS

ANTIQUES ASSOCIATIONS

BADA *(The British Antique Dealers'
Association)*
20 Rutland Gate
London
SW7 1BD
Tel: 0207 589 4128
Fax: 0207 581 9083
www.bada.org

*LAPADA (The Association of Art &
Antiques Dealers)*
535 King's Road
Chelsea
SW10 0SZ
Tel: 0207 823 3511
Fax: 0207 823 3523
www.lapada.co.uk

ANTIQUES AND COLLECTABLE CENTRES

Alfie's Antique Market
13-25 Church Street
Marylebone
London
NW8 8DT
Tel: 0207 723 6066

Aladdin's Cave
188 Woodlands Road
Charing Cross
Glasgow
Scotland
G3 6LL
Tel: 01413 325757

Battlesbridge Antiques Centre
The Old Granary
Hawk Hill
Battlesbridge
Essex
SS11 7RE
Tel: 01268 561700

Brecon Antiques Centre
22a High Street
Brecon
Powys
Wales
LD3 7LA
Tel: 01874 623355

Grays Antique Markets
58 Davies Street
Mayfair
London
W1K 5LP
Tel: 0207 629 7034

Herts & Essex Antiques Centre
The Maltings
Station Road
Sawbridgeworth
Hertfordshire
CM21 9JX
Tel: 01279 722044

The Old Warehouse Antiques
7 Delamere Street
Chester
Cheshire
CH1 4DS
Tel: 01244 383942

Sheffield Antiques Centre
178–88 Broadfield Road
Sheffield
South Yorkshire
S8 0XL
Tel: 01142 584994

The Antiques Centre York
Allenby House
41 Stonegate
York
Yorkshire
YO1 8AW
Tel: 01904 635888

ANTIQUE FAIR ORGANISATIONS

Devon County Antiques Fairs
www.antiques-fairs.com
Email: dcaf@antiques-fairs.com

DMG Antiques Fairs
PO Box 100
Newark
Notts
NG24 1DJ
Tel: 01636 702326
www.dmgantiquefairs.com

AUCTION HOUSES

Abbey Antiques
Lyde Court
Hereford
HR1 3AE
Tel: 01432 357753
Fax: 01432 261284
www.abbey-antiques.com

Bamfords
Matlock Auction Gallery
133 Dale Road
Matlock
Derbyshire
DE4 3LU
Tel: 01629 57460

BBR Auctions
Elsecar Heritage Centre
Barnsley
South Yorkshire
S74 8HJ

Tel: 01226 745156
www.onlinebbr.com

Bonhams
101 New Bond Street
London
W1S 1SR
Tel: 0207 629 6602
Fax: 0207 629 8876
www.bonhams.co.uk

Bonhams Edinburgh
65 George Street
Edinburgh
Scotland
EH2 2JL
Tel: 01312 252266

Christie's
85 Old Brompton Road
London
SW7 3LD
Tel: 0207 930 6074
Fax: 0207 752 3321
www.christies.com

Henry Aldridge & Son
Unit 1 Bath Road Business Centre
Bath Road
Devizes
Wiltshire
England
SN10 1XA
Tel: 01380 729199
Fax: 01380 730073
www.henry-aldridge.co.uk

Newport Auctions Ltd
The Auction House
Usk Way
Newport
South Wales
NP20 2BX
Tel: 01633 262626

Saltburn Salerooms
Diamond Street
Saltburn-by-Sea
North Yorkshire
TS12 1EB
Tel: 01287 622360
www.saltburnsalerooms.com

Sotheby's
34–35 New Bond Street
London
W1A 2AA
Tel: 0207 293 5000
www.sothebys.com

Thomas Watson
The Gallery Saleroom
Northumberland Street
Darlington
DL3 7HJ
Tel: 01325 462559
www.thomaswatson.com

Vectis Auctions Limited (Toy
Collectables)
Fleck Way
Thornaby
Stockton-on-Tees
TS17 9JZ
Tel: 01642 750616
Fax: 01642 769478
www.vectis.co.uk

Wellers Auctioneers
70 Guildford Street
Chertsey
Surrey
KT16 9BB
Tel: 01932 568678
Fax: 01932 568626
Email: auctions@wellers.co.uk
www.wellers-auctions.co.uk

BOOK DEALERS
Peter Harrington Books
100 Fulham Road
Chelsea
London
SW3 6HS
Tel: 0207 591 0220
Fax: 0207 225 7054
www.peter-harrington-books.com

COLLECTABLES COMPANIES
Bears 'N' Bunnies
Upper Thames Walk
Bluewater

Kent
DA9 9SR
Tel: 01322 624997
www.bearsnbunnies.com

Lorna Bailey Artware
The Old Post Office
12 Wedgwood Street
Burslem
Stoke-on-Trent
ST6 4JH
Tel: 01782 837341
www.lorna-bailey.co.uk

Merrythought Ltd
Ironbridge
Telford
Shropshire
TF8 7NJ
Tel: 01952 433116
Fax: 01952 432054
www.merrythought.co.uk

Millennium Collectables
PO Box 146
Newark
Nottinghamshire
England
NG24 2WR
Tel: 01636 703075
Fax: 01636 702372
www.millenniumcollectables.co.uk

Portia (Doulton and Beswick
Specialists)
The House of Portia
23 Boleyn Way
Hainault
Essex
IG6 2TW
Tel: 0208 500 3505
Fax: 0208 500 2707
www.portia.co.uk

Raleigh UK Limited
Church Street
Eastwood
Nottingham
Nottinghamshire
NG16 3HT
Tel: 01773 532600

Royal Doulton plc
Sir Henry Doulton House
Forge Lane
Etruria
Stoke-on-Trent
ST1 5NN
Tel: 01782 404045
Fax: 01782 404254
www.royaldoulton.co.uk

Teddy Bears of Witney
99 High Street
Witney
Oxfordshire
OX28 6HY
Tel: 01993 702616 or 706616
Fax: 01993 702344
www.teddybears.co.uk

UKI Ceramics Direct Limited
Tel: 0208 500 0345
www.coalport-snowman.co.uk

INFORMATION
Antiques Trade Gazette (has index
of dealers and auction houses all
over the country)
www.antiquestradegazette.com

BBC Website
www.bbc.co.uk/antiques

Disposal Service
Freephone: 0800 390000
www.mustdestroy.com

Google Search Engine
www.google.co.uk

Wickedlady Collectables (Advertising items, tins, film memorabilia)
www.wickedlady.com

20th Century Decorative Arts
www.20thcentury-decorative-
arts.co.uk

INSURANCE
Hiscox Insurance
Tel: 0845 345 1666
www.hiscox.com

Antiques Information Service
PO Box 93
Broadstairs
Kent
CT10 3YR
Tel: 01843 862069
Fax: 01843 862014
www.householdinsurancenow.com/
art-antiques.insurance

Connoisseur Policies
Suite C
South House
21-37 South Street
Dorking
Surrey
RH4 2JZ
Tel: 01306 734600
www.connoisseurpolicies.com

Michael James and Associates
159 Shirley Road
Croydon
Surrey
CR0 8SS
Tel: 0208 655 3504
Fax: 0208 656 8424
www.mjacollections.co.uk

MUSEUMS AND GALLERIES
Museum of Childhood
Cambridge Heath Road
Bethnal Green
London
E2 9PA
Tel: 0208 980 2415
Fax: 0208 983 5225
www.museumofchildhood.org.uk

Victoria and Albert Museum
South Kensington
Cromwell Road
London
SW7 2RL
Tel: 0207 942 2000
www.vam.ac.uk